D0699020

Especially for

Sue

From

Joan

Date

Christmas 2013

Christmas 2013
Old friends are best friends.
Here is ta a very Best friend.
Joan Westcott

The
Quilt
of Life

A Patchwork of
Inspirational Thoughts

The Quilt of Life

A Patchwork of
Inspirational Thoughts

Mary Tatem

BARBOUR
PUBLISHING

Published by Barbour Publishing, Inc., P.O. Box 719, Uhrichsville, OH 44683, www.barbourbooks.com

Our mission is to publish and distribute inspirational products offering exceptional value and biblical encouragement to the masses.

 Member of the
Evangelical Christian
Publishers Association

Printed in China.

Dedication

To my mother,
Louisa Griner McCormick,
who taught me at an early age that
God establishes patterns for
His people's lives.
She was an inspiring example
of maintaining a thankful
heart as we follow
His design for us.

Acknowledgments

I want to thank the many gracious people who shared their stories about quilts with me.
I'd especially like to thank Nancy Gloss, the owner of Nancy's Calico Patch, and Mary Frances Ballard, both of whom patiently answered my questions and supplied resources for my research. A large thank-you goes to my son, Andrew Tatem, who gave his time and skill to critique the book.

Contents

Welcome to the Warmth of Quilts

Quilts wrap our hearts in warm emotions. They represent time, energy, and planning. The hours required to create a quilt offer plenty of opportunity to think about the person for whom it is intended. When combining needlework with prayer, a quilter catches a glimpse of the love of God, who stitches the fabric of our lives with His plans and purposes for our good and not our destruction.

A quilt bridges the generation gap by connecting people from the past with people yet to come. Perhaps that longing to participate in the future gives quilting its strong appeal. A quilt represents a reach for immortality. We stitch hoping our lives, our personalities, our struggles, and our joys will find a place of remembrance in the minds and emotions of others.

While reading these pages, tap into the heartbeat of our Creator, the Master quilter, who designs our lives using His perfect pattern. Skillfully placing the lights and darks of our lives, He joins the mountains and valleys of our days to make us into comforters who warm others.

Relax with this book for a few moments each week, allowing the thread of God's truths to beautify and stabilize your life while you become God's work of art.

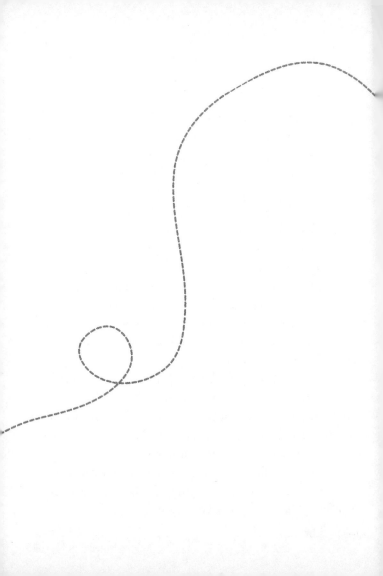

Surprise Changes

> "Give, and it will be given to you. A good measure,
> pressed down, shaken together and running over,
> will be poured into your lap. For with the measure
> you use, it will be measured to you."
>
> LUKE 6:38 NIV

One only needed to step inside the scarred front door of the middle school to feel the poverty and neglect of the youngsters who attended it. In this school, learning and sharing were not priorities. The children's days were dedicated to defending their rights. In the middle of this discouraging environment, Mary Fran tried day after day to teach home economics. No one cared. One day she arrived in class carrying a huge shopping bag full of colorful fabric scraps. When she dumped them on the table, curious eighth graders crowded around.

"Has anyone ever heard of safe houses for battered women?" she asked. They had. Some even spoke of relatives who had spent time in one of these havens for women who, beaten by husbands or boyfriends, feared for their lives.

"I'm looking for volunteers to make quilts to put on the beds at a battered women's safe house. I'm hoping these quilts will warm and comfort some women who are afraid and in despair."

To Mary Fran's delight, four girls and one boy volunteered. They enjoyed selecting bright and cheerful prints from the piles of donated materials. Their teacher marveled at the conscientious efforts her students made to cut even squares. The room buzzed with excitement the day they laid the squares out on tables to decide what arrangement of the various colors and patterns looked best. After a few suggestions, the students were careful not to put all the red tones at one end and all the yellows at the other. For the first time in their lives, they were striving for artistry. Next, they used serger machines at the school to stitch the squares together into five quilts. As the squares of the top were sewn to the backing and batting material, they chattered with pride over their attractive quilts. The children enjoyed a rare sense of accomplishment.

> **TIP**
> Before washing fabric, use the serger sewing machine to stitch the edges of your material to prevent fraying.

The following morning, Mary Fran arrived in her classroom to discover someone had stolen one quilt overnight.

She dreaded telling the class. The group of kids who had so far only exhibited a "what's in it for me" attitude amazed her with their response. The children agreed with a girl who said, "Well, if someone took it, maybe they really needed a quilt to keep them warm and show them some people care about what happens to other people."

When we use God's pattern for living, God often gives us surprising little twists of benefits beyond what we expected. By giving to others, these thirteen-year-old children shook off their "me first or I get even" attitude to develop an important character trait—generosity. They learned to consider the needs of others ahead of their own desires. When we give to God, He returns to us growth and maturity.

God's Pattern
When we practice giving to others,
God changes us,
and we gain the unexpected blessing of
receiving extra joy as we become more like Christ.

The Unexpected

*For I know the thoughts that I think toward you,
saith the LORD, thoughts of peace, and not of evil,
to give you an expected end.*
JEREMIAH 29:11 KJV

Anne breathed in the sweet smell of powder mixed with clean baby. She gave the soft, round bottom a quick pat before she fastened her new daughter's diaper. She snuggled the baby close, reveling in motherhood. Her joy dimmed only a moment at the thought that had haunted her the entire nine months of her pregnancy. How could a mother give up her little child? Anne's mother had done just that: She had left her husband and then three-year-old Anne to find a life of "fun," so the story went.

"I'll never abandon you, little one," Anne murmured as she laid the sleeping baby in her crib. "I'll always make sure you know I'm glad you were born."

A short time later, the doorbell rang, and the postman

handed Anne a bulky package. Her heart leaped at the return address. She had never received anything from her mother's address. Her throat squeezed and tears threatened. If she had cried for her mama long ago, she didn't remember it anymore. All she ever felt was an empty place, one of not quite belonging in spite of all the love her father and aunts and uncles had given her.

Slowly she snipped the tape and pulled the paper away to reveal a worn, somewhat faded baby quilt. Pinned to it was a note that read: "This was made for you when you were born, by my mother, your grandmother. I wanted you to have it for your new baby. Mother."

Anne spread the quilt over the nearby table. She fingered the carefully embroidered animals in each corner of the lovely blending of pink fabrics. Tears mingled with laughter

TIP
To store an old quilt, use a prewashed white pillowcase.

as she looked at her grandmother's handiwork. Someone had rejoiced she was born after all. Her grandmother cared enough to spend hours cutting, piecing, and sewing little pieces of fabric into a pretty design to celebrate her birth. She could picture a gray-headed lady sitting in a rocker stitching love into the fabric. Anne hugged the quilt to herself and danced around the room singing her own made-up little tune. "Someone was glad I was born. Someone was glad."

Smiling, she tiptoed into the baby's room and gently laid the quilt over the sleeping form. Her daughter stretched a minute and then settled back to sleep. "I'm glad you are here, little one. When I wrap you in this quilt, I'll remember someone cared about me."

No one is unwanted by God. Even before our birth, He cared about us. His love for His people is constant and never fails. He has wrapped us in His love even when we don't feel it. "But the plans of the Lord stand firm forever, the purposes of his heart through all generations" (Psalm 33:11 NIV).

God's Pattern
Even if a person feels unwanted,
God has a special plan for every life.

Galloping Horses

You, then, why do you judge your brother or sister? Or why do you treat them with contempt? For we will all stand before God's judgment seat.
ROMANS 14:10 NIV

I would never have stuck to quilting if it weren't for my Grandma Brown." Laura stood by her quilt hung at the quilt festival. "My other grandmother, Grandma Winters, always won first prize in quilt competitions. If she didn't think it was good enough to win, she didn't enter it. She demanded perfection from herself, ripping out and reworking so she could win. As a child I didn't notice the subtle differences that made one quilt win over another.

"'Grandma, let me stitch a little on your quilt,' I'd ask, but I was always given a different square for practice. Then Grandma checked it and turned it over to examine the stitches on the back, clucking her tongue all the while. She'd hand it back to me, telling me to rip it out and do it again. I spent more time ripping than sewing at her house. I hated it.

"But at Grandma Brown's house, she'd look at my work and call out to my mother or Grandpa, 'Will you look at Laura's quilting! She improves every day. Why, I declare, she is becoming a little seamstress.'

"When I'd get discouraged because the points and edges of my pieces weren't matching up exactly right, she'd dismiss the problem with a wave of her hand saying, 'You'll never notice it on the back of a galloping horse.'"

> **TIP**
> Because of the chemical process of manufacturing silk, it rots faster than other material. Avoid silk if you want a lasting quilt.

Isn't that a wonderful way for us to look at the flaws in each other? Why point out the problems a person has? They are probably painfully aware of them anyway. If we dwell on another's faults, we forget to notice his or her good qualities, and we may become discouraged from offering them friendship and acceptance. As we gallop through our days, life goes too fast to waste time criticizing. Let's concentrate on noticing the improvements and strengths in everyone. Encouraging words create growth and determination to improve.

God's Pattern

God is a perfect judge. He understands all
the facets of our behavior and responses. His bountiful
mercy balances His judgment.

Wondering Why They Wander

These commandments that I give you today are to be upon your hearts. Impress them on your children. Talk about them when you sit at home and when you walk along the road, when you lie down and when you get up.
DEUTERONOMY 6:6–7 NIV

Years ago in the United States, a quilt pattern called Wandering Foot enjoyed popularity because its attractive design was relatively easy to piece. Later a folktale linked the pattern with rebellious children leaving home much earlier than expected. Searching for explanations for why their children left, disappointed parents began to blame the comforter dubbed Wandering Foot for their heartache. Eventually the superstition developed that if a child slept under a Wandering Foot quilt, the boy or girl would leave home at a young age. Understandably this pattern lost its appeal and was studiously avoided until some clever person renamed the pattern Turkey Tracks. The new name was associated with a common sight in rural America, removing the fears surrounding the motif, and the design enjoyed a renewal of favor. Kids could once again safely snuggle under its warm cover.

Christian parents rely on God's protective cover over their youngsters rather than troubling themselves with superstitions. They gear their daily conversations to include

TIP

For small quilts, hold the three layers of the top, batting, and backing together with lots of safety pins instead of basting thread to keep them from "wandering" apart.

instructions about God. Any actions or events of the day are appropriate moments to reinforce the knowledge of God and His plans. By steady example and training, parents surround their children with God's designs for successful living. Even when a child is rebellious and makes poor choices, a parent who has taught his or her children about God's love finds peace. We know that, ultimately, God will fulfill the promise of scripture: "Start children off on the way they should go, and even when they are old they will not turn from it" (Proverbs 22:6 NIV).

God's Pattern

The family is God's plan for teaching each new generation about His ways. When we trust God to help us raise our children, we are not tormented by superstitions.

Ownership

"Do not fear, for I have redeemed you;
I have summoned you by name; you are mine."
ISAIAH 43:1 NIV

"Where's your name? Didn't you sign this wonderful quilt?" Beth asked Marie as she helped examine the quilt for any remnants of basting threads.

"I didn't think I would."

"Why not? Aren't you proud of it? You should be. It's a beautiful quilt, and you sure invested enough time in it. How long did it take to finish all this handwork?"

"Three years. I *am* proud of it; I know it's not perfect, but it's pretty."

Beth showed Marie a book full of lovely drawings for quilt labels. Marie traced one on a piece of muslin and colored the design with permanent-ink colored pens. Next she wrote her name, the date and place she completed the quilt, the reason she made it, and the name of the person she was giving it to.

"Your label will matter to someone a couple of generations from now," Beth said with satisfaction while Marie slip-stitched it to the back of the quilt at one corner. "This quilt says something about you. It's a piece of your history. I hope you're proud of your careful workmanship. Anyone would feel proud to own this quilt."

We are the careful workmanship of God, who created us. And He is pleased with His creation. We are not perfect, but He loves us anyway because He made us. He wants to polish what He made and make us more beautiful each day.

TIP

Attach your quilt label on the back before you quilt the layers together. The quilt stitches will integrate the label into the project and prevent anyone from removing it later.

When we allow Him to arrange the pieces of our lives, His plan, His pattern for us is more perfect than anything we can create on our own. The Bible tell us that He knows us so well He even knows how many hairs we have; yet He gladly proclaims His ownership of us and calls us by our name.

Isaiah 49:16 (NIV) says: "See, I have engraved you on the palms of my hands; your walls are ever before me." He writes His name on us when we accept Christ, and we are called by His name when we are called Christians, which means "little Christ."

◇※◇※◇※◇

God's Pattern

God loves us even when we know we have not
pleased Him. He does not tire of working with
us and nudging us toward completion.

Alarm Buzzers

"*But if you do warn the righteous person not to sin
and they do not sin, they will surely live because
they took warning, and you will have saved yourself.*"
EZEKIEL 3:21 NIV

Diane's heels clicked across the floor. Her pace mirrored her excitement. "Unbelievable!" she exclaimed as she entered the huge room in the museum where dozens of Baltimore Album quilts hung in grand display. "The colors are gorgeous." Her exclamation of delight was lost on the burly guard who stood stone faced at the door. Together with her sister-in-law, Betty, Diane approached the first magnificent quilt.

"Look at the amount of tiny, close stitching." As Diane leaned nearer to examine the craftsmanship, a loud buzzer rang. Startled, Diane jumped back and looked at the guard who was glaring at her.

"Imagine doing this intricate needlework without

electric lighting," Diane commented as she read the date for the next quilt. Keeping her hands carefully behind her back so the guard would see she knew better than to touch the valuable collection, she moved closer to study the work. Another raucous buzz rang through the room.

"What was that?" Diane asked, bewildered. She noted the guard added a frown to his glare.

"Maybe the museum is testing a new burglar alarm. I don't think that guard likes us," Betty whispered as they moved on.

The women walked from one quilt to the next, awed by the workmanship and beauty. Over and over they were puzzled as the buzzer rang. The guard kept moving closer to them.

"I wish I had brought the magnifying glass I usually keep in my purse," Diane commented. "Then I could see the stitches even better." The buzzer blared again.

"I think I'm glad you didn't." Betty began to giggle. "I've figured it out. That alarm rings whenever you lean close to a quilt. The museum is protecting their treasures from damage. Can you imagine what it would sound like in here if you pulled out a magnifying glass? The guard would probably think you were going to catch the rays from the skylights and set the thing on fire."

Red faced, Diane finished her tour of the quilts at a respectful, but visually frustrating, distance.

The world offers many attractive or exciting sights and activities, including an afternoon enjoying a quilt collection. Sometimes the activities are good but provide an undesirable distraction from more important pursuits. Some pleasures are actually harmful for us. Leaning too close to these temptations will endanger us. God wants to protect us from damage more than any museum wants

TIP
At quilt shows, the staff handles quilts with white gloves to prevent soiling the items. Wearing clean white gloves is a good way to handle any precious heirloom quilts we own.

to protect its quilt collection. When we throw ourselves into busy days with too much hustle and bustle, our time with God becomes crowded out. That communication with God is what keeps us alert to His warning buzzer.

God's Pattern
God's warnings often come in quiet thoughts.
We must listen to hear them above the clamor of our day.

Magic Quilts

He is despised and rejected of men; a man of sorrows,
and acquainted with grief: and we hid as it were our faces
from him; he was despised, and we esteemed him not.
ISAIAH 53:3 KJV

"Camp Magic, the name's a joke! I don't see the magic of sitting around a campfire crying about our son. I must have been insane when I let you talk me into coming this week." Chad's jaw muscles tightened as he struggled to stuff down his emotions.

"Give it a chance." Jeanne wiped her eyes with an already damp tissue.

"No chance of letting this program turn me into a blubbering mess like you and these other people. No way! I didn't even know these kids they lost, and nothing we do here can bring a single child back to life. Our Chuck is gone, and we just have to go on."

"We can go on as if we're really living if we let ourselves

find healthy ways to express our grief." Jeanne's voice dropped to a whisper of despair at the frozen expression on her husband's face.

She smiled in gratitude when Grant, a burly construction worker, grabbed Chad's arm after lunch and propelled him over to the horseshoe pit.

Moist with perspiration, Chad joined her later in the lodge for the afternoon program.

TIP
When painting or writing on fabric, check to make sure that the paints are permanent and won't wash out. Ironing helps set fabric paint.

"Grant's boy was the same age as ours when he died. It was an auto accident," Chad informed her as he sat down at a long table. Each couple was handed a muslin square and given instructions to paint a picture that reminded them of their deceased child. As Chad snorted and flung the material at his wife, Grant slid into a chair beside him.

"I wonder if we'll make a quilt out of our pictures like we did last year." Grant pointed to a comforter hanging at one end of the lodge. "My square is the one with the tent on it. Brad would jump up and down with excitement when I'd set it up in the backyard. The memories were so painful; I thought I'd die painting that picture. But, you know, afterward when I told last year's group why the tent represented a piece of Brad's life, the memory made me feel better. Whenever I volunteer at the counseling office and see my square hanging there, I remember the happy times with my son and the healing deepens.

"This year I want to paint a tricycle. Brad loved charging up and down the driveway on his red trike. I'm not much good at drawing. Since you're an engineer, do you think you could help me sketch a tricycle on this?" He tossed his material in front of Chad.

After he'd penciled in a trike for Grant, Chad turned to Jeanne. "Do you think a red wagon would represent our good times with Chuckie?"

Jeanne blinked back her tears. "Oh, Chad, it helps me so much to hear that you remember them."

"I know. I guess I thought if I didn't talk about him, somehow I could avoid dealing with the pain of his death. Maybe this quilt is magic after all," Chad mumbled into Jeanne's hair.

Our Lord understands our grief. He knows the depth of pain we experience when we suffer any kind of loss. Since He is always with us, we are never alone in our sorrow. Meeting with others who have experienced the same kind of grief helps us cope. When we fellowship with people who have suffered loss, the fact that someone else can still enjoy life after a tragedy encourages and strengthens us to rise above the suffering.

God's Pattern

God allows us to help others in the same way
He helped us when we were in sorrow.

Homesick

O God, thou art my God; early will I seek thee:
my soul thirsteth for thee, my flesh longeth for
thee in a dry and thirsty land, where no water is.
PSALM 63:1 KJV

Bet you can't guess what I brought you from town," Bart called to Carrie, who stood in their shanty doorway. He pulled his team of horses to a stop in front of the water trough before he slid off the wagon seat. While the horses slurped the water, he strode to the shanty door, keeping one arm behind his back.

"Is it a licorice stick?" Carrie threw her arms around her husband's neck. "You didn't have to bring me anything. I'm just glad you're home. It's so lonely when you are gone. Not another soul to talk to. I started talking to the pigs."

"I know it's lonely out here." Bart stroked her hair. "Maybe next time I won't have to detour and hunt for missing cattle. Then I'll take you to town with me when

I go for supplies. Believe me, you were more comfortable here in the shade of our home." He wiped the sweat from his forehead with his sleeve, bringing his other arm around into view.

"A package!" Carrie squealed with delight.

"Hey, the pigs do talk to you." Bart laughed when the animals set up an answering commotion in their pen. "The postmaster said it arrived a week ago, but nobody was riding down this way." Bart handed her the package and, putting an arm around her waist, ducked under the lintel of the doorway.

She carefully untied the string and unfolded the brown wrapping paper, smoothing it for future

> **TIP**
> Old scraps work well for patterns that suggest antiquity because they have been used for centuries.

use as she went. "Look! A letter from Ma and one from Elsie." She set them aside to unwrap another packet. "Fabric scraps." Carrie's voice rose with excitement. "This must be a piece from Elsie's wedding gown." She held up a large swatch of delicate lawn fabric, dotted with tiny pink rosebuds. A sketch of her sister's dress was pinned to the material. "This is the next best thing to seeing her wear it." She blinked back tears as she examined the drawing. "These pleats would have emphasized Elsie's tiny waist.

Oh, Bart can you picture what a beautiful bride she was?"

She pulled out a piece of pink cotton with a lilac print. Next, she found a sturdy chunk of light blue gingham. She read the note pinned to it: " 'This was the backing the neighbors used when they quilted Elsie's wedding comforter.' "

"With these scraps I'll have enough material to complete my basket quilt top next winter when the weather traps us inside. Instead of feeling sorry for myself, I'll spend days quilting and thinking about my sister and how happy she must be as a new bride. Only this morning I asked for God's help to endure the winter."

"Don't forget I'm here with you." Bart nuzzled her hair and pulled a licorice stick out of his shirt pocket.

"And you do know how to sweeten the environment." Carrie took the candy and offered her lips in a kiss of thanks.

In the days before photographs were common, women sent clothing scraps as a form of information and a way to keep family ties strong. The pioneer women who settled our West experienced a "dry and thirsty land" in both their physical environment and their isolation from others and separation from loved ones. Clinging to God was the pathway to maintaining emotional health in difficult situations, as it is today. "For he satisfies the thirsty and fills the hungry with good things" (Psalm 107:9 NIV).

◇◇◇◇◇◇◇

God's Pattern

He is faithful to supply a spiritual feast
to help us in our places of isolation.

Complete Joy

*Fulfil ye my joy, that ye be likeminded, having the same love,
being of one accord, of one mind.*
PHILIPPIANS 2:2 KJV

Nancy's excitement grew with each package the mailman brought to her door. Several months earlier she had suggested an ambitious project to her college friends now graduated and scattered to their individual lives. The group of girls had developed close friendships during their enrollment at Virginia Tech. For four years, they lived, played, and studied together. Their many opportunities to unite in worship seemed to cement their friendships more than any other activity.

Now, Susan, Nancy's college roommate, was planning her wedding. As a gift suggestion, Nancy asked each of the friends to make a quilt square that represented an aspect of their campus life together. Nancy undertook the job of putting the pieces together and doing the final quilting for the present. Every arrival of a finished contribution in the mail brought a smile. Nancy relished the creativity of her friends. One cross-stitched a map of Virginia and highlighted the location of the campus, every girl's hometown, and the bride's and groom's birthplaces. The square stenciled with penguins brought a giggle and an almost forgotten memory of the bride's affection for the funny-looking birds. One of the patches was appliquéd with symbols of teaching since Susan studied for that profession. The squares represented a nice selection of crafts. In addition to the appliqué, cross-stitch, and stenciling, there was candlewicking and freehand painting with appropriate sayings stitched upon them.

Nancy alternated the four-cornered fabric with heart appliqués of a pink printed fabric to create a cohesive design. For Nancy, the time she spent putting the finished quilt pieces together revived pleasant memories. She relished the love poured into each square as evidenced by the care taken for each design. The classmates were still "all in one accord" giving time and thought to make something that would bless their friend. The joys of friendship and shared activities, dreams, hopes, giggles, and tears were resurrected in the quilt.

As the deadline drew near, the pressure mounted, but the work remained a complete joy. Knowing her friends' eagerness to continue their friendship despite their separation made the stitching worthwhile.

More than material possessions or even exciting experiences, our relationships bring us the most joy in life. Maintaining friendships requires effort. Relationships are cemented by shared experiences, laughter, dreams, and thoughts. The greatest joy of all comes from our relationship with God. Fellowship with God offers the highest kind of joy available to us on this earth. As human friendships are birthed with the investment of

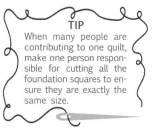

TIP
When many people are contributing to one quilt, make one person responsible for cutting all the foundation squares to ensure they are exactly the same size.

our time, energy, and thought, we develop our friendship with God in the same way. Find time to converse with our heavenly Father. Delve into His love letter to us, the Bible. Develop the habit of listening for His voice with your heart.

God's Pattern

When we share our hopes and dreams with our heavenly Father and cement our friendship with God by making time for Him in our daily lives, He will stitch joy into our lives.

Hear My Cry

A thousand shall fall at thy side, and ten thousand at thy right hand; but it shall not come nigh thee.
PSALM 91:7 KJV

"It's a hideous war." Tina's needle paused over the pink and gray tulip she was stitching to her muslin background. She sat with her mother close to the fireplace.

Her mother picked up a pile of pink flower petals cut from worn-out curtains. "I agree. All war is hideous, so why are you using your brother's Confederate army uniform in your quilt?" She shuddered. "It's a gruesome reminder of the nurses cutting it off of him when he was wounded."

"I don't think of Robert; I think about Jim when I see the gray. I remember how handsome he looked in his uniform as he marched away to battle." Her vision blurred, and her stitching paused. "To think Jim and I would be married next month if he wasn't rotting away in a Yankee prison up north." She wiped her eyes. "When will this miserable war ever end? You'd think they could let a man go to get married," she said, poking her needle through the material with an angry stab.

"They don't want Jim shooting at them again, sis. Be glad he's not crippled." Tina turned at Robert's voice. With only a remnant of a limp, he had abandoned his cane, eager to rejoin the Southern forces.

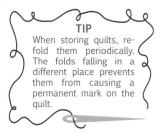

TIP
When storing quilts, refold them periodically. The folds falling in a different place prevents them from causing a permanent mark on the quilt.

She was thankful for Robert's recovery, and she thanked God every day for keeping Jim from permanent harm in the battle. But she hated the feeling that her life had halted in the middle of a sentence, as if every part of her life was holding its breath waiting for Jim to return, waiting for the war to end before motion would return to her world. She stitched faster on the quilt top. Her lips moved in quiet prayer for Jim's safety. As she stitched and prayed, the peace of God stole into her heart.

"I know what Bible verse I'm going to embroider on this quilt," Tina told her brother. "The one that tells us a thousand may fall on your left or right, but you will not fall. I think it's Psalm 91. Making this quilt is keeping me from going absolutely mad with worry about Jim."

Many quilts are preserved in collections bearing silent witness to the timeless occupation of women who, through their needles, expressed their fears and love for their sweethearts, husbands, and brothers caught up in the destructive forces of war. Quilts made during the Revolutionary War, the Civil War, the War of 1812, as well as World War I and World War II hang in museums to remind us of the human cost of our nation's freedom. Patterns of eagles, symbols of the United States, and names of soldiers were blended with scripture verses as women implored God for the safety of their loved ones.

Throughout the history of North America, women have drawn strength to endure separation, danger, and fears by studying the Bible and grasping the comfort of the God we learn about from it.

God's Pattern
None of our heartaches take God by surprise.
He knows when and how much help to
send us in our times of trouble.

Mile after Mile

Know ye not that they which run in a race run all, but one receiveth the prize? So run, that ye may obtain.
1 Corinthians 9:24 KJV

John blinked his eyes and slapped his thighs. His horse jerked to the right, breaking his steady pace. "Good boy. Wake me up a little. I don't want to fall asleep and tumble out of the saddle."

John didn't relish the hundred-mile ride from his homestead into town so soon after his last trip for supplies. He swatted flies with his hat before wiping the perspiration from his forehead. Days of travel through miles of woods alternating with meadows heated by the midsummer sun stood between him and the general store in Junaue County, Illinois. He patted his horse's neck as he spoke. "Someday this land will bustle with people, then you and I will have a less monotonous ride into town. We'll probably have some other towns a whole lot closer to our stake."

When at last the wood frame stores loomed into view

on the horizon, John straightened in the saddle and went over his shopping list in his mind. He pulled to a stop in front of the general store and tied the reins to the rail.

"Need nails or tools already?" The storekeeper looked surprised to see John.

"I'll get some nails later, Stefan," John told the storekeeper. "Need to look at your calico bolts first off. That's the main reason I made the trip so soon. Need to keep the little woman happy, you know." Feeling like the proverbial bull in a china closet, he fingered the material. "Wish I could have brought Ellie, but she's too near her time to jostle a hundred miles on a horse. She'd know better which colors go with what. That's a pretty pink flower on that cloth. Do you think it would blend with this purple stuff in a quilt?" He fished in a pocket and brought out a four-inch swatch of a lavender print.

"Ha!" Stefan laid the bolt on the counter. "Ask me about galvanized tin and things like that. I don't know anything about matching up colors. Let me see if Maizy can step away from her bread making long enough to help." In a moment, Maizy followed Stefan from the family quarters behind the store, wiping the flour off her hands onto her apron.

"Ellie wants to finish this quilt she's making before the

baby comes, but she had her heart set on making a border that matches all the way around instead of patching scraps together." John ducked his head. "Things like that get kinda important to a woman, you know, all alone out there with a first baby coming."

"I know." The wail of an infant penetrated the partition behind the counter. "This green print is soft, and it won't matter if the baby is a boy or a girl with lavender

TIP
When the quilting process seems long, think about something pleasant to make the time pass faster. Try contemplating the character of God.

and green blended together." Maizy pulled a length off the bolt and set John's scrap on top of it. "Mighty nice of you to make the trip just for calico for Ellie." She patted John's arm.

"Now don't be saying I came all the way to town just for cloth." John shifted, and red began to rise from his collar and cover his face. "We can use some sugar and some of those nails Stefan mentioned."

"You must be swinging your hammer all day long if you already used up the nails I sold you last time." Stefan couldn't resist the jab at his friend.

"Getting ready for another mouth in the house, you know." John paid for his purchases and hurried to his horse before he took any more joshing about making a long journey for quilting cloth. John hardly noticed when the sun succumbed to clouds and sprinkles of rain cooled the land. Instead he pictured his Ellie, her hair tied back with a ribbon, opening the package of pale green calico.

It was common in pioneering days for the early settlers pushing toward the West to need to travel long miles to secure any supplies. Pretty new fabric was a luxury many women did not have. More than one pioneer man plied his way over tedious miles to bring his wife such a prize.

Sometimes the race God sets before us in life is quick and fascinating. Sometimes it is slow and monotonous. Either way, if we set our minds to obey God and do what He desires of us, there is a prize at the end of the race. When weariness tempts us to quit, we focus our minds on our love for God. The strength to finish comes from God Himself. The desire to please God motivates us to continue our efforts.

God's Pattern
God rewards our perseverance.
He calls us to the race; He equips us to do it well;
and then He rewards us for doing it.

Source of Power

"Don't be alarmed," he said. "You are looking for Jesus the Nazarene, who was crucified. He has risen! He is not here. See the place where they laid him."

MARK 16:6 NIV

Kim shuddered when she looked at the wall hangings that hung in the museum. Centuries old, the pictures made by the Fon people of West Africa didn't make her think of feeling safe and cozy wrapped up in a quilt in front of a warm fireplace. The appliquéd pictures represented the violence of battle scenes. The works bristled with weapons in the hands of broad, angry-looking men.

Kim drew back at a grisly picture of an execution. Hardly what she'd choose to hang in her house, although the bright colors were pleasing from a distance. A sign told Kim the pieces were not made by women busy nurturing their young. Only men from the court tailors' guild of Fon, West Africa, made these pictures. This art form came from warriors making hangings to proclaim their power and authority. In their culture, winning wars was highly valued. The wall hangings were symbols of power. The irregular, asymmetrical designs also sported many brightly colored animals intended to convey the wealth of the warrior. The men who translated triumphant war stories into appliquéd wall hangings enjoyed important status in their society.

Even as Kim stood grimacing at the needlework, she realized a battle raged for power and authority in her own life. Week after week she struggled to write reports for her bosses that pictured her as winning whatever the current contract required. While she didn't write about executing her competition, she did cut them down to picture herself as a victor. Reports that slandered others made her company's division look good.

TIP

Machine quilting is a good way to overcome time pressures. The machine gives a more distinct indentation. If the material ripples, adjust the pressure.

The picture of Christ hanging on the cross came to her mind. He had chosen an infamous death so she could live. Then He conquered death and rose again. Right there in the museum, Kim breathed a prayer of surrender to God. If He could die and rise again for her salvation, His resurrected life could flow through her to help her at her work. She did not need to disparage others to come out ahead. She needed to ask for His power to perform her tasks. She determined to rely on His strength instead of her own.

God's Pattern

Contrary to the instinct of man to maintain authority
by demonstrating power to our adversaries,
Christ died and, to man's surprise, arose again.
His death brought victory over His enemy and ours.
"The LORD shall fight for you, and ye shall hold your
peace" (Exodus 14:14 KJV). The NIV translation reads:
"The LORD will fight for you; you need only to be still."
When we still our hearts before God, He will fight for us.

When Push Comes to Shore

Yea doubtless, and I count all things but loss for the
excellency of the knowledge of Christ Jesus my Lord:
for whom I have suffered the loss of all things,
and do count them but dung, that I may win Christ.
PHILIPPIANS 3:8 KJV

"Ouch." Twelve-year-old Debbie jerked her left hand out from under the quilt she was working on. "I keep sticking my finger when I push the needle up from underneath the way you showed me. I hate this. It's no fun."

"A few finger pricks go with quilting. You said you like my quilt"—Mother paused and held up her own nearly finished wall hanging—"and you'll like yours, too, when you see a little more progress. The Sunbonnet is a simple pattern for a beginner. You're the one who asked to learn, remember?"

"I didn't know it meant poking myself to death." Debbie sucked her third finger. "Look, it's bleeding. Now

I'll get blood all over my sunbonnet girl."

"Quilting requires a little practice, just like any other skill we try to master. Here, let's put a bandage on your finger." Mother wrapped the adhesive around Debbie's finger. "It'll help two ways—stop the bleeding and give you a little cushion in case the needle finds your finger again when you push the fabric up to make a tiny stitch.

> **TIP**
> Pushing the fabric from underneath helps the needle take a smaller bite and keeps the stitches smaller.

Eventually quilters get a callus on the finger they work with underneath the quilt. Look at me." Mother held her left hand up to Debbie's face. "See how tough the skin is on the one I use to put the pressure on the quilt? But the pressure is part of the reason I won the quilt prize at the county fair. Pressure helps me make tiny stitches. Look. I can get six to ten stitches every inch."

"Who cares?" Debbie frowned.

"It never hurts to strive for excellence. You don't need to be perfect, but you can keep pressing yourself to improve."

"Just let me do it the easy way. I get tired of pressure. It never stops at school. Somebody is always making fun of me when I try to act like a Christian. Anna made fun of me today because I chose Cindy to play on our softball team. She isn't as good as the others, but I felt sorry for her and didn't want to leave her out. Anna said she'd quit the team and join another one if I kept Cindy. If Anna quits, we'll lose every game because she's the star player."

"Sounds to me like you are letting the pressure make an excellent Christian out of you. I'll bet Anna's words pricked as badly as your needle did."

"Made me mad, but I don't care if we do lose. I don't want to hurt my friend's feelings."

"That's the way. Allow God to use the pressure to make you into a beautiful Christian." Mother hugged Debbie. "Loyalty to a friend is a whole lot more important than making a beautiful quilt. Maybe Cindy will take an interest in Jesus the next time you talk about Him."

When the pressures of life create heavy burdens and the pricks of a cruel world leave us stinging, we can turn to God and ask Him to help us grow under the press of our trials. He knows just how much pressure to allow into our lives. God's workmanship in us causes our lives to bless others and attracts them to our Savior. "But the God of all grace, who hath called us unto his eternal glory by Christ Jesus, after that ye have suffered a while, make you perfect, stablish, strengthen, settle you" (1 Peter 5:10 KJV).

God's Pattern

When we turn to God in the midst of suffering,
He strengthens us. A settled peace is one pattern
God stitches into our lives when we turn to Him
for the strength to survive the pressures of living.

Paying the Price

Verily, verily, I say unto you, except a corn of wheat
fall into the ground and die, it abideth alone:
but if it die, it bringeth forth much fruit.
JOHN 12:24 KJV

The Revolution was far from Jane McCrea's mind early Sunday morning in July 1777, when she ran the brush through her thick, long hair one last time before picking up a bucket and heading for the gate of Fort Edward, New York. Excitement brought a bounce to her step and a lilt to her voice as she greeted a fort guard.

With the water she would fetch from the spring, she planned to freshen herself and fix breakfast. She had looked forward to this day when she would wed her handsome British lieutenant and become Mrs. David Jones. Her wedding thoughts interfered with her accustomed alertness when she was outside of the strong fort walls. In an instant her shivers of delight turned into a tremble of terror when a small group of Indians leaped from the brush at the spring.

The last sight Jane saw on what was supposed to be her wedding day was an Indian's sweaty arm held high above his dark scowl. His tomahawk swiftly descended to separate her lush, lovely hair from her vibrant head and transport her quickly to Christ, her heavenly bridegroom, instead of her earthly one.

His wedding so dominated Lieutenant David Jones's thoughts that morning when he reported to British General John Burgoyne, he found it hard to concentrate on business. Even the arrival of a band of Indians failed to gain his attention until the leader of the group threw a scalp on Burgoyne's floor.

"Aha." The general reached into his camp desk and handed the Indian some silver coins, commenting that this would help discourage the citizens from supporting the revolutionary cause.

For a long moment, David Jones stood transfixed. He had run his fingers through Jane's thick flowing hair too often not to recognize the scalp belonging to his beloved. He turned on his heel and left the tent and the camp, hurrying toward the fort.

The news spread rapidly. Jane McCrea was killed on her wedding day. General Burgoyne was buying scalps to weaken his opposition. He thought the people would see they needed the British and stop rebelling against England. The reaction of the people was the opposite of what the general expected. Thousands of horrified men volunteered to join the colonial ranks. The colonial forces, weak in number and poor in supplies, suddenly swelled to numbers made formidable by determination born of outrage. Even Burgoyne's followers faltered in support of him. He met military defeat at nearby Saratoga; and, two months later when he surrendered, many taunted him by chanting Jane McCrea's name. Newspaper articles decried his actions, songs were sung heralding Jane as a heroine of the Revolution, paintings were displayed, and the colonists rallied to what they perceived to be a righteous cause.

TIP
For perfect matching when machine sewing, use very fine pins and sew over them.

Many quilts are inspired by heroes and heroines. One depicting scenes from Jane's life on the front and with her story written on the back won a prize at a quilting show held in Williamsburg, Virginia, in 1997. The depth of emotion in the story as well as the quality of the work stopped every passerby.

The outrageous loss of Jane McCrea's life on a day

meant for blissful joy fills us with regret. Who could have guessed that God would take this terrible tragedy and use it as the turning point to help colonial America establish independence from England?

God's Pattern

Many times we are confused by the turbulence of our lives, but God sees beyond our limited understanding and knows what serves His best and highest purposes. "And we know that all things work together for good to them that love God, to them who are the called according to his purpose" (Romans 8:28 KJV).

Sweet Memories

He hath made his wonderful works to
be remembered: the LORD is gracious
and full of compassion.
PSALM 111:4 KJV

G randma, we have the best present. It's—" Four-year-
old Kaitlyn squirmed when her mother clapped a
hand over her mouth, stopping her eager disclosure before
she ran up the steps into her grandparents' house.

"Don't tell the secret, Kaitlyn. You don't want to spoil
the surprise. We have to wait until all the aunts, uncles, and
cousins arrive before we give Grandma and Grandpa their
anniversary present. Here, carry the rolls in." Noreen handed
the bag to her daughter in a vain effort to distract her.

"You can't guess what we're bringing, Grandma."
Kaitlyn pointed to the bulky package her father carried into
the house and deposited on the coffee table.

"Whatever could be so big it needed yards of pretty

gift paper to wrap it?" Grandma's eyes twinkled at Kaitlyn.

"We all look pretty on—"

"Kaitlyn, go play with Casey before you give the whole thing away." Noreen took Kaitlyn by the shoulder and steered her into the family room where her cousin, Casey, held out a doll to her.

"Here, dress your doll up for Grandma's anniversary party." Satisfied her daughter was safely distracted from blabbing about the family gift, Noreen returned to the car to unload her portion of the festive dinner the Brandts' four daughters had prepared for their parents' fiftieth anniversary.

TIP
Many photocopy shops do an excellent job of transferring photographs to fabric.

Even Noreen fidgeted with anticipation long before the last van drove up to unload the final group of the family. "Let's give them the present before we eat," she whispered to her sister as she helped her unload the car and shepherd the children inside to join their cousins. "I don't think I can keep Kaitlyn from spilling the beans for a whole meal."

The family gathered with cameras in hand while the honored couple sat on the sofa and began to carefully peel away the tape from the package.

"You're too slow." Kaitlyn reached out an eager hand

to help. "Tear it, Grandpa."

After a satisfying rip, a unique gift of love lay on the Brandts' laps. Murmurs of delight filled the room. Photographs of each family member were photocopied onto fabric squares and then combined to make a quilt commemorating the entire span of the Brandts' marriage. Grandma and Grandpa held up the large quilt filled with pictures of the most important treasures of their lifetime: their offspring. In the center was a reproduction of their wedding picture from fifty years ago. Around the center, every child was represented on the quilt by more than one picture, ranging from their babyhood to adulthood. The grandchildren also were represented in their various stages of growth.

Cameras clicked to record the surprise; and, moments later, they recorded the tears of joy coursing down the Brandts' faces. Sniffling, Noreen passed around a box of tissue. "Don't cry on the quilt. After all, it's an heirloom."

Before the small children could ask why everyone was crying about the perfect present, joyful voices filled the room with sometimes humorous, sometimes poignant stories as one after another, the family recalled memories triggered by the quilt of pictures.

Happy memories warm our hearts as thoroughly as

quilts warm our bodies from the chill of a winter evening. Remembering the blessings God has poured into our lives revitalizes our faith and bolsters our joy. Make a conscious effort to stay grateful to God, not only because of what He has done for us, but because He is perfect and pure. Our faith grows when we remember His graciousness toward us.

God's Pattern

God's compassion is endless in our lives. He builds joy into our hearts when we remember His goodness.

Down in the Dumps

Who redeemeth thy life from destruction;
who crowneth thee with lovingkindness
and tender mercies.

PSALM 103:4 KJV

Sherry put on rubber gloves and headed out the back door to the Dumpster between her yard and the shirt factory behind her house. She carried an empty shopping bag over her arm, a broomstick in one hand, and a kitchen stool in the other one.

"Let's see what treasures I find today," she told the calico cat who ran out to greet her when she plopped her chrome stool against the blue side of the Dumpster. The cat purred, rubbing her orange fur against Sherry's ankles. She leaned the broomstick against the Dumpster, pulled a chicken bone wrapped in aluminum foil out of her pocket, and placed it on the ground for the animal.

"You and I have a lot in common, Callie." Sherry

scratched the cat's ears before she climbed on the stool and peered into the Dumpster. "We both scrounge around for scraps to make ends meet. The mortgage company, however, isn't likely to throw *me* a bone.

"Ah, looks like the good old shirt factory has several nice bones for me today." Sherry lifted a large piece of material out with her broomstick. "It's the perfect red to back my Pinwheel top." Callie meowed as if to rejoice with her. "I've a customer willing to pay good money when I finish the Pinwheel quilt."

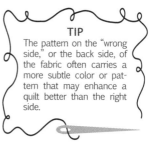

TIP
The pattern on the "wrong side," or the back side, of the fabric often carries a more subtle color or pattern that may enhance a quilt better than the right side.

She held it up to the light. "Callie, can you understand why they threw away a piece big enough to make shirts for an entire ball team? I wouldn't think this funny yellow line down the side is reason enough. Goodness, any self-respecting seamstress could cut that away and use the rest. The dried soda pop will wash out fine." She folded the fabric and tucked it into her shopping bag.

In response, the stray cat growled over its bone. "You'll have to wait until tomorrow for the other chicken leg. Sorry, it's just one scrap at a time from my table."

But the Dumpster yielded a better return. She stirred at the piles of scraps, discarded cardboard, and empty plastic bottles with her broomstick. "A perfect baby blue check." She lifted the material up on her broomstick. "I'll use this for the new baby line I'm making for the consignment store."

Callie purred. "You're right about that." Sherry nodded to the cat. "Pretty good pickings today."

Sherry snared some smaller brown and yellow scraps on her broom and shook them off into her bag. "Good for my Flying Geese pattern." She retrieved a few more pieces of solid blues before climbing down. "If it doesn't rain and the garbage pickup doesn't come extra early, I'll come back and sift through the bin again tomorrow and bring you the other bone. Gracious, I might celebrate tonight by eating some extra chicken and bring you the wishbone tomorrow.

"Some folks might not like the view of this big old Dumpster in their backyard, but the good Lord put it here for me."

Sherry patted the cat one more time then picked up the kitchen stool and walked to her back door. She gave a satisfied wave of her hand to the cat and went straight to her sewing machine to make as much progress on her quilts as she could in the remaining daylight.

When we feel down in the dumps, God has the means and the desire to rescue us. Whether it is in an unorthodox manner like Sherry, maintaining the supplies for her quilting business from the throwaways of a shirt factory, or a more standard route to provision, God provides our needs. When we turn to Him, He also supplies us with emotional insights to improve our lives.

God's Pattern

He takes the refuse of our lives and forms it into
a useful pattern that accomplishes valuable results.

A Gorgeous Sight

Let the beauty of the LORD our God be upon us:
and establish thou the work of our hands upon us;
yea, the work of our hands establish thou it.
PSALM 90:17 KJV

Rosemarie could hardly take in the beauty of the quilt. She wouldn't argue with the judges who hung a large blue first-place ribbon prominently above the breathtaking work. A flourishing flower garden filled the wall hanging. Hundreds of flowers fashioned from tiny bits of fabric splashed across the width of the quilt. Each flower was identifiable and contained two or more colors that combined to make the flower appear almost real.

Awed by the intricate work, Rosemarie wondered how many hours it took to piece together such a masterpiece. The craftsmanship and artistry of the piece before her made her own quilt tops look like the work of a kindergarten student. Even the garden wall was sewn with each brick individually fashioned and nestled close to the next one. Subtle color changes brought depth as the wall curved away. The breathtaking beauty lifted her mind off of her trials for the moment.

Beauty does that. It offers a tiny respite of pleasure in the midst of life's difficulties. It's never a waste of time to acquire the skills required to create a splash of beauty in a

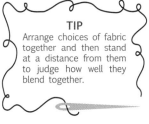

TIP
Arrange choices of fabric together and then stand at a distance from them to judge how well they blend together.

world full of trouble and evil. Beauty is the nature of God Himself. A lovely creation in any artistic form reminds us of the God who created the ones who perform the artwork. While Rosemarie looked at the magnificent creativity of a woman who was only a name on a quilt show label, she thought about the creativity of her Lord, who was the ultimate Master craftsman of her life and of all the lives of her loved ones.

When Rosemarie came to the quilt show, her heart felt heavy with concern over her five-month-old grandson who lay in a hospital, fighting for his life. If God Almighty could inspire and enable a woman to create such a gorgeous sight as the quilt that hung before her, He could inspire and enable the doctors and nurses who were searching for causes and cures to restore her grandson's health.

Beauty inspires us to look more closely at the God we love. Seeing the beauty of God helps us better understand the depth and breadth of His love. The more we know God, the more we see His beauty and the beauty He creates in our lives even in the midst of troubles we do not understand. We come to appreciate God for Himself, beyond what He does for us. Psalm 27:4 (KJV) tells us: "One thing have I desired of the LORD, that will I seek after; that I may dwell in the house of the LORD all the days of my life, to behold the beauty of the LORD, and to enquire in his temple."

God's Pattern

When we recognize God is the creator of beauty, we understand the source of our own creativity. Ecclesiastes 3:11 (NIV) tells us: "He has made everything beautiful in its time. He has also set eternity in the human heart; yet no one can fathom what God has done from beginning to end."

The Substitute

> But God commendeth his love toward us, in that,
> while we were yet sinners, Christ died for us.
> ROMANS 5:8 KJV

"Did you make this quilt?"

Ruth smiled when she answered. "No, my friend Jill made it."

"Tell Jill it's a beautiful work of art," the lady in the blue suit said. "I love lots of roses on comforters." She leaned closer to look at the stitches. "Your friend did a lovely job."

"If you'll let me take your picture, you can help me tell Jill." Ruth laid down her pad on which she had written the woman's comments and picked up a camera. "My friend is in the hospital recovering from surgery for cancer. She's so disappointed she can't be here. I know she would enjoy the wonderful response her quilt is receiving at the quilt show. I'm standing in for her today and recording all the nice things people say and taking some pictures of people admiring her quilt so she will feel like she participated in the excitement, at least in a small way."

"How thoughtful." The lady squinted at Ruth's name tag. "Didn't I see a quilt with your name hanging in the exhibit?"

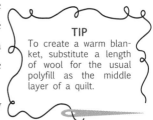

TIP
To create a warm blanket, substitute a length of wool for the usual polyfill as the middle layer of a quilt.

"Yes, but it's not nearly as exquisite as this one."

"People may be saying nice things about your quilt."

"Never mind. I really want to be here."

Over and over for the full three days of the quilt show, Ruth wrote down the words of admiration people spoke when they looked at the rose quilt. Her camera recorded the moment when the judges hung an honorable mention on the piece. No one in her quilter's guild had ever won a ribbon at a show before.

When Ruth went to retrieve her own quilt at the end of the show, she was dumbfounded to find another honorable mention ribbon hanging by it. She didn't say a word about her own award when she took her notepad and pictures straight from a one-hour developing store to her friend's hospital bed.

"Look. You won a ribbon." Ruth pinned the yellow ribbon onto her friend's nightgown. "Everyone loved your quilt. Listen to the things people said." A big smile watered with tears decorated her friend's face while Ruth read page after page of enthusiastic praise for Jill's pretty comforter. Jill recognized lots of women from her quilt guild in the pictures, but she found great satisfaction in the number of strangers who complimented her quilt. They had no reason to make nice remarks about her work unless they genuinely admired it.

Ruth took her sick friend's place at the quilt show to allow her to participate in a small way. She willingly sacrificed enjoying the rewards of her own quilt. Because of her, Jill enjoyed some of the pleasures of a triumphant day. Jesus Christ took our place on the cross in order to allow us the privilege of entering into eternal life. His sacrifice was the ultimate one of substituting His life and blood for our sins.

◇◇◇◇◇◇◇

God's Pattern

God designed a way for us to enjoy the triumph
of Jesus Christ over sin and death, which allows
us to live with Him forever and ever.

Hiding Place

*Thou art my hiding place; thou shalt preserve
me from trouble; thou shalt compass me
about with songs of deliverance. Selah.*
PSALM 32:7 KJV

Who's the man riding in front of those soldiers?"
Calvin asked his friend, Joseph Wadsworth, as they
stood together in front of the Hartford house of legislation
in the Connecticut colony.

"Bad news for freedom, that's who. He's Sir Edmund
Andros, whom King James II appointed governor over the
Dominion of New England." Joseph raised his chin and
set his jaw in a firm line. "Can't be in Connecticut's best
interest for him to arrive in town. In 1675, his troops came
into Saybrook and seized the fort.

"Thank God for feisty citizens loyal to the Connecticut
colony." The local schoolmaster pounded his right fist into
his left palm. "They put up such resistance, the troops rode

out again. Afraid of a little bleeding, I guess."

"Let's hope Connecticut doesn't shed any blood because of this visit. We aren't going to stand for loss of freedom in 1687, any more than we did twelve years ago," Calvin said.

> **TIP**
> To hide a knot, tug it through the top of the quilt and into the batting.

Later in the day, Calvin stood outside an open window and listened to the hot words tumbling from the legislators' meeting room.

"The charter represents our freedom. We will never surrender it."

"The king of England gave the charter to John Winthrop for the Connecticut colony in 1662, and we won't give it up." Voices blended together in protest against Sir Edmund Andros.

Every time he heard Joseph's voice ring out for freedom, Calvin swelled with pride for his friend. The debate raged on until most of the listeners standing outside drifted home for a late dinner, but the passionate talk continued. Calvin hoped his wife would understand why he wanted to stay and listen. Their entire way of life was at stake.

When the light faded, the dissension did not. The

men in the chamber lit several candles so they could make notes and read the expressions on their fellow legislators' faces. Some of the men were ready to turn the charter over. Occasionally fingers reached for the document on the table as if to take possession of the paper for their point of view.

A strong gust of wind stormed up the street. It blew Calvin's hat off as it swept inside the room and extinguished the candles. As Calvin fumbled for his hat in the street, he felt someone brush past him. A moment later the candles were relit, and Sir Edmund Andros's bellow of rage pierced the air. The charter was gone.

Calvin turned and quickly followed the shadowy figure who had brushed past him to a nearby grove of large oak trees. Even in the dark, Calvin recognized the profile of Joseph Wadsworth. He was close enough to see his friend pull a paper from his coat and stuff it into a hole in a large oak tree. Sir Edmund Andros could not seize a paper that had disappeared.

One year later Sir Edmund Andros's rule ended when King James II lost power in England. Soon afterward, Calvin's wife, Dorcas, and other women began stitching a new quilting pattern of four green oak leaves arranged in a circle and connected by eight brown acorns. The women, who called the pattern the Charter Oak quilt, made it as a reminder of freedom in Connecticut.

God stands ready to protect us in times of danger. He knows the best way to hide us from trouble. Sometimes we aren't aware of the danger or His protection. In addition to hiding us from trouble with our earthly enemies, He defends us from the archenemy, Satan, who desires to destroy us. He also understands our need for emotional protection. We can ask Him to protect our lives in every realm—physical, emotional, and spiritual.

God's Pattern

God values our freedom to choose to follow after Him.
He allows us to decide how much we will trust Him.
He helps us grow strong enough to lean on His
divine wisdom instead of our feelings.

Pure Loveliness

But as he which hath called you is holy,
so be ye holy in all manner of conversation.
1 PETER 1:15 KJV

Did you hear what Ruby said about Liz yesterday?"
Gertie cupped her hand beside her mouth as she
spoke.

"No, what?" Viva raised her head from her quilting.

"You won't believe me when you hear. It's a juicy
story." Gertie's eyes glinted with mischief.

Gertie leaned closer to Viva and lowered her voice.
Instead of going unnoticed by the members of the quilting
group, the furtive conversation drew attention. Needles
stilled and all eyes turned to Gertie. She straightened up in
her seat as red crept into her face.

"Tell us, too, Gertie. Must be some tale," Sable called
out.

"Let's turn on some more lights in this room. I'm

having trouble seeing my work," said Beth, trying to change the subject. "This white stitching on white material requires good eyesight. Maybe my eyes are too old to attempt it."

"It's worth the effort. The serene elegance of pure white creates a lovely quilt," Halley said, understanding what Beth wanted to do.

"It reminds me of purity, which is why I chose it for a bridal gift."

TIP
White fabric or paper behind the eye of a needle makes it easier to see when threading it.

"Come on, Gertie, out with your story." Sable was not distracted.

"Let's not," Beth said, keeping her voice calm. "Remember when we started meeting we determined to only speak well of one another."

"This isn't about us. It's someone else." Gertie tried to defend herself.

"I guess conversation is like your quilt, Beth; even a few stitches of another color would spoil the pure loveliness of the work," Halley spoke up, and, after an awkward pause, the conversation moved on to more uplifting topics.

Instead of listening to gossip about others, we can turn a conversation to a less destructive direction by changing the subject. When we refuse to listen to gossip, we become instruments God uses to demonstrate righteousness. Bringing Jesus into a conversation ushers His light into it since Jesus is the light of the world. Where His presence is, it becomes uncomfortable to gossip.

God's Pattern

Purity of conversation is God's design. "Only let your conversation be as it becometh the gospel of Christ: that whether I come and see you, or else be absent, I may hear of your affairs, that ye stand fast in one spirit, with one mind striving together for the faith of the gospel" (Philippians 1:27 KJV).

Bulletproof Vests

He shall cover thee with his feathers,
and under his wings shalt thou trust:
his truth shall be thy shield and buckler.
PSALM 91:4 KJV

As James packed a change of clothes in his saddlebag, ivory arms slid around his waist from behind. Dropping the bag, James smiled and grabbed Glenda's hands. Twisting around, he cupped her chin in his hand. "I'll miss you, my little posy."

"Make haste and rout the Anglo-Saxons, then hurry back to me safe and sound. My life holds still until you return." Glenda pursed her lips into a pout.

"We'll only find minor skirmishes on our foray. The Battle of Hastings won the big war for William the Conqueror. When we suppress these local rebellions, I'll have my steed at a gallop for you."

Glenda wrapped her arms around his neck. "Did you

notice that my seamstress mended the tear your angry hound made in the quilted clothing? I can't help but wonder if a hound can cause a tear, what would a lance do when thrown from a racing steed? Will it protect your heart?"

"It's my skill which protects my skin, but the thick fabric takes the brunt of a glancing blow from a dagger or arrow." He kissed the tip

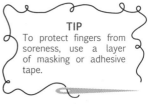

TIP
To protect fingers from soreness, use a layer of masking or adhesive tape.

of her nose. "I'm well motivated to dodge all the weapons and return. You've provided me with excellent protection with closely quilted, thick clothing."

Early in the history of warfare, man began searching for techniques to improve his safety. The warriors of the eleventh century used quilted fabric as armor worn under their chain mail in an effort to provide some additional protection from the dangers of battle.

God provides His believers with a wrap of protection against the dangers of our battles, whether they are physical, spiritual, or emotional. The entire ninety-first Psalm speaks of His protection for us. When we read about the protection of His feathers, we think of a mother hen's feathers. She clucks to call her chicks when she wants to hide them from danger under her wings. When we heed the call of God and run under His will, we experience His protection. God's protection is available to us when we run from the world's standards to hide ourselves under His love.

God's Pattern

When we align our choices with His will,
which we find in the scriptures,
God's technique is to wrap us in His protection.

Hands On

Though he fall, he shall not be utterly cast down:
for the LORD upholdeth him with his hand.
PSALM 37:24 KJV

"I want yellow."

"I want mine blue."

"Will this paint wash off? Yuck. I don't want a green hand all summer."

"Is there enough red paint for my handprint?"

The kindergarten classroom buzzed with the excitement of five-year-old voices enthusiastic about their project to honor their teacher, Mrs. Mason. Since the teacher's baby was born two weeks early, she would miss the final weeks of school with her class. The room mothers took advantage of her absence to plan a surprise for the teacher who had won their admiration for her gentle and yet thorough preparation of her students for first grade.

"Can I put both hands on the quilt to show Mrs.

Mason I love her?"

"Then I get to put my footprint on, too, because I love her that much."

The children responded with enthusiasm to the idea of making a quilt of their handprints for their teacher.

One by one, each child walked to the front of the class where their room mothers stood gripping eager wrists to control how much and where the paint landed. After pressing a handprint onto the large muslin piece stretched across several tables, the room mother kept a tight hold on the wiggly child until she dunked the paint-layered hands in a washbasin of sudsy water. Even with their best efforts, clothing and assorted classroom fixtures received unplanned decoration.

Before snack break, the material carried twenty colorful handprints, each one with a name scrawled underneath in childish handwriting.

"Tomorrow, when the paint is dry, you will each help with the sewing to make this top into a quilt," the substitute teacher promised before the children lined up to go home.

Before school the next day, busy mothers arranged the painted top over batting and a backing. Each child was allowed to choose a color of heavy yarn, and the mothers resisted the urge to laugh at the pursed lips, stuck-out tongues, and other grimaces the children made threading their blunt, big-eyed needles.

"Don't I sew good, teacher?" The curly blond girl beamed with pride when her stitch succeeded in going through all three layers and back up to the top where she tied a knot and cut the thread. She bit her tongue as she concentrated. The mothers' backs ached from a morning of bending over to help position stitches and determine if the needle went through all the layers, not to mention ensuring the scissors cut only thread, not material.

As a good teacher, Mrs. Mason had left her

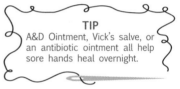

TIP
A&D Ointment, Vick's salve, or an antibiotic ointment all help sore hands heal overnight.

handprint on each child's life as she diligently prepared the students for their future schooling. Teachers, parents, and even people with only casual contact imprint our children's personalities and character, bringing some impact to the children's future decisions. When we are with children, we must bear in mind that our words and actions are placing a print on their lives as surely as if we put a paint-laden hand upon them. Children prosper with adults who take care to provide good influences in their lives.

God's Pattern

God holds us in His hand and keeps His hand on us. When praying for the children in your life, ask God to keep His hand upon them to direct their ways. Pray they don't fall away from God and ask Him to pick them up and restore them when they do. Be alert for the opportunities we have to represent the hand of God and influence little ones to believe in Him. "And the hand of the Lord was with them: and a great number believed, and turned unto the Lord" (Acts 11:21 KJV).

Where's Home?

*Thou wilt shew me the path of life:
in thy presence is fulness of joy; at thy
right hand there are pleasures for evermore.*
PSALM 16:11 KJV

I liked our house in Virginia better," Kara whined as the Johnsons' car stopped behind the moving van in the driveway of the family's new house.

"You'll have a bigger room all to yourself in this house." Mother kept her voice cheerful.

"I'll share a room with Kara if I can move back to Virginia. Texas doesn't have any trees. Virginia's better," Rachel agreed with her younger sister.

"The Air Force needs Daddy to live in San Antonio for a while. And there are, too, trees. There's one right in our front yard."

"Not lots of trees like Virginia." Kara stuffed her thumb in her mouth.

"We'll have a good time finding out what fun things we can do in our new state." Loraine Johnson's patience was wearing thin.

"It's not fun if I can't play with Tammy." Rachel's pout matched Kara's. "She's not in Texas."

Mother sighed. "I know you miss your friend, but you'll meet some wonderful new ones here. Let's go inside and see if the movers have set up your beds."

TIP
Be open to trying new techniques and equipment.

"I'll get lost at night trying to find the bathroom," Kara complained as the girls trailed behind their mother up the stairs to find their father.

To Loraine's relief, the furniture in both the girls' rooms was in place. "Here's the box marked sheets and quilts," Loraine said. "Let's make your beds first thing."

The girls grabbed their quilts with glad cries when Mother pulled them from the carton.

Kara lay down on her bed after her mother spread the quilt over the clean sheets and smiled. "It's fun to be by myself," she said as her sister and mother stepped across the hall to make Rachel's bed.

"It feels like home now," Rachel said. "I love my doggy quilt."

Loraine Johnson sighed with relief at the difference in her girls' attitudes. They began to explore their new house with enthusiasm instead of complaints.

On future moves, the first item of business for this military family was to set up and make the girls' beds. Somehow the presence of their quilts on a familiar piece of furniture established security for the children and smoothed the way for adjustments.

When we sense God's presence in our lives, we enjoy a secure feeling and adjust to the changes life brings. Since change is one of the guarantees of life, we need to learn to find His presence and become comfortable in it. His presence helps us adjust to the unexpected.

God's Pattern

To maintain the flexibility we require in life,
we need to learn how to enjoy God's presence.
The time we spend in prayer, reading the Bible,
and meditating on the character of God and
His nature will help us feel at home and
comfortable in His presence no matter
how our surroundings change.

Free Indeed

And ye shall know the truth,
and the truth shall make you free.
JOHN 8:32 KJV

Caroline slipped her handkerchief from her pocket. Turning her head, she dabbed at her eyes, hoping none of the women noticed. As she slid the hankie into her bodice, she looked around. Every head was down with each woman scrutinizing her own stitching. *This is the last time I try to work on Reggie's freedom quilt in front of other people. I can't seem to help crying over it.* Caroline straightened her shoulders.

"Is this Reggie's freedom quilt, Caroline?" Melody leaned over to examine the eagles marching around the edge of the blanket.

Caroline sighed. "It seems impossible, but he'll be twenty-one before the year is over. I want to finish his freedom quilt for his birthday in November. How fast the years have flown."

"You have a lot of Bible verses on his quilt." Melody pointed to the one from Proverbs which warned young men to heed God's instruction.

"I keep thinking of important verses I want him to remember as he makes the serious decisions of life. Now that he's grown, I can't follow him around and whisper good advice in his ear, but he'll take his quilt with him when he leaves home. Maybe it will remind him of his Christian heritage and keep him on the right path." Caroline clutched the quilt to her heart.

Melody sighed. "I can't imagine what I'll do when my Tommy leaves. In only ten years he'll be twenty-one."

"Make him a freedom quilt when the time comes. The warmth it provides is probably less important than what making it does for a mother's peace of mind. I find myself praying the scriptures I embroider for him with stitches of love. By the time I finish making the comforter, I hope my heart understands what my mind already knows—Reggie is not my little boy any longer. He's a man. The freedom quilt represents the gift of independence his father and I grant him on his twenty-first birthday."

"That sounds too final for me." Melody shook her head.

"Why do you think I have to stop so often and wipe away the tears?" Caroline pulled her hankie out again. "Until Reggie turns his own son loose someday, he won't appreciate how much of a sacrifice it is to let him go. Oh, he'll go on loving us. Maybe he'll come and ask advice sometimes, but it won't be the same as rocking away the hurts of a little boy, or dusting off grass and leaves from my skirt after a spontaneous hug." She finished embroidering the words *Holy Bible* on the front of the large black rectangle in the center of the quilt. "I'm letting him go, but I hope the quilt will remind him of what I taught him."

TIP

Relax your hands, arms, and shoulders when doing free motion quilting on a machine. This allows a creative flow of fabric under the needle and encourages evenly spaced stitches.

A custom for some women in the latter part of the nineteenth century and early twentieth century was to make a quilt for their sons' twenty-first birthday that acknowledged that the boy was now an independent man, free from the restraints of his mother. Judging from the amount of scripture used on some of these quilts, the mothers hoped their sons would use their independence to serve Christ.

Real freedom comes from allowing Christ to cleanse

us from sin. The truth of the gospel provides a permanent source of liberating freedom. Some young adults think independence from the rules and expectations of parents or society provides liberty, but they later discover this freedom only leads to consequences they had not expected. The freedom that follows a clear conscience brings a liberty beyond the understanding of people without Christ.

God's Pattern

God intended the instructions of the Bible
to bring us the freedom of clean hearts instead
of blind bondage to a list of do's and don'ts.

I'll Cut the Sheet

I will not leave you comfortless:
I will come to you.
John 14:18 kjv

The pressure of unshed tears behind Cheryl's eyes sent shooting stabs of pain through her sinuses as she adjusted the blanket around her sleeping baby. With one finger, she traced the outline of one of the Raggedy Ann dolls decorating the flannel.

"Mama will make you a cake tomorrow for your first birthday," Cheryl whispered. "I'll make it in the shape of a doll just like the pictures on your blanket. Think how good the icing will taste." She listened to Brook's shallow breathing. "Can you hold on for one more day, precious girl?" She stroked her baby's cheek, searching for even a tiny trace of color in the pale face.

"I take that back." She cradled her daughter close. "You don't have to struggle to live anymore. I release you to God." Still, the tears didn't flow.

In the agony of the months that followed Brook's death, the gray-laden skies of winter matched the despair in Cheryl's heart. "Even the clouds don't rain!" she shouted one time at the sky. Her grief seemed dammed up inside.

People tried to help, and Cheryl went through the motions of living. She bought groceries and cooked meals that tasted like sawdust. She accepted invitations for lunch and made polite noises in response to her friends' chatter. Everything she did was as if it were happening in a thick fog, a cloud of pain that hovered over her life. Nowhere did the sun shine in her soul.

TIP
Sharp scissors help cutting accuracy.

"I've got to get on with my life." She watched her husband try to reach her and finally draw away from the rebuff of indifference. Only the pictures of Brook with her first birthday cake brought her any comfort. Brook had smiled at the bright colors and smacked her thin lips over tiny tastes of icing. Cheryl never regretted making the elaborate cake for her baby, although she was much too ill to eat it.

"Got a good idea," Cheryl's friend Dina announced, standing on her doorstep. "Put on your lipstick; we're going to visit the quilting guild that meets in my church every month."

"I don't quilt."

"Neither do I, but we both sewed layettes when our babies were coming. I'm guessing we might like quilting." Dina was persistent, and Cheryl's detached state made it easier to go along placidly with her friend's efforts to help.

The projects the women stitched at the meeting piqued her interest. When she watched the day's demonstration of appliqué, she grasped an idea. At home she rummaged through the box of baby things her husband had packed away until she found the Raggedy Ann blanket. She laid out a length of muslin her friend provided and picked up a pair of scissors. After a moment's hesitation, she clenched her teeth and cut a slash into the flannel up to the closest Raggedy Ann picture. As she cut around the doll's edges, her vision blurred with a cascade of tears. She laid down the scissors and sobbed, releasing her grief in great torrents.

Over and over she repeated the process, cutting out a doll and then crying as if her heart would break. Instead of breaking, however, she began to feel a touch of healing. She ironed under the edges and, one by one, stitched the dolls onto her muslin.

Slowly, as the project progressed, smiles accompanied her stitching as often as tears. She began to recall the happy times with Brook: her first tooth, her giggles when Daddy tickled her, and the crooked smile over her first birth-day cake.

"Your top's ready to quilt," the ladies at the quilting guild encouraged her, happy to see the luster restored in their friend's eye, and her enthusiasm for life returning. "What are you going to use for the backing?"

"I thought one of Brook's crib sheets would make a good backing."

"Perfect," Dina agreed.

At the next meeting, everyone was surprised to see Cheryl with a different project. "Did you finish your Raggedy Ann quilt?" Dina asked.

"No, I couldn't cut the sheet. I just couldn't."

The ladies changed the subject. Laughter bounced around the room as usual when the women gathered. At the end of the meeting, Cheryl, whose silence had lasted the entire meeting, spoke up. "Your friendships and quilting have helped me heal. I'm going to cut the sheet and finish my quilt. The Raggedy Ann pictures bring good memories. I want to see them hanging in my house."

God has a way to bring healing for the grief of each

sorrow in our lives. He sent the Holy Spirit to bring us comfort. God understands the pain we experience in life, and His heart is touched by our sorrow.

God's Pattern

He does not leave us alone in despair but provides
a way to healing. The act of creating helps us tune
into our great Creator and open up for His comfort.

What?

And he called his ten servants, and delivered them ten pounds, and said unto them, Occupy till I come.
LUKE 19:13 KJV

"Please, please, let me sew!" Jasmine tugged at her mother's arm.

"Let go, Jasmine. You're going to make my stitches crooked. After you turn seven, I'll let you sew. Right now I have the perfect job for a five-year-old. When the ladies go home from our quilting bee, you can pick up all the threads and little pieces of material that fall on the floor."

"That's no fun. Let me cut." Jasmine picked up a nearby pair of scissors and whacked the air, alarming the nearest lady who ducked out of the way.

"You have to be even older to do the cutting." Mother removed the scissors before her daughter could hurt someone with them. "If the pieces aren't cut exactly right, the pattern won't fit together correctly."

Soon Jasmine tired of watching the ladies and wandered off to play with her dolls.

Her interest in quilts was long forgotten by the time her mother called her to come help clean up.

"Please pick up all the trash and put it in here." Mother gave her a paper bag and pointed out the threads and scraps littering the floor under the quilting frame.

"I don't wanna. I wanna help make the pretty cover."

"Picking up these threads is the right size job for you. Look how hard it is for your big mama to crawl around under the frame." Mother dropped to her knees and demonstrated her tight fit underneath.

Jasmine laughed.

"See. Your fingers are just the right size to pick up the threads. My fingers are too big and have to try several times before I finally grab a thread."

Jasmine plucked up a thread.

"Good girl. Get your fingers trained for picking up, and you'll be ready to sew before you know it."

Jasmine's new job was to pick up, and pick up she did. It didn't take Jasmine long to

TIP
A magnet attached to a long handle helps pick up pins from the floor.

figure out complaining wouldn't win her a reprieve. She

eventually made it into a game by pretending she was a bird finding material to build a nest.

"Look, Jasmine, I bought you a printed quilt square to sew and learn to make even stitches." A brown bunny stood in the center of the material Mother gave her. Around the edges blue, yellow, and green shapes formed the borders. "You've been so good at the clean-up task, I believe you're ready for a more grown-up stage."

How many times do we fret over chores that seem insignificant to us? God is pleased when we accomplish the small jobs as well as the ones we deem important. What seems unimportant to us, God views as a stepping-stone of preparation for larger responsibility. In Matthew 25:21 (KJV) we read: "His lord said unto him, Well done, thou good and faithful servant: thou hast been faithful over a few things, I will make thee ruler over many things: enter thou into the joy of thy lord." In God's training program, the small acts come before the bigger things.

God's Pattern

God wants us to fill our time with worthwhile activities that He directs. His plan is for us to occupy ourselves for the advancement of the Kingdom.

A Cold, Dank Cell

*"I needed clothes and you clothed me,
I was sick and you looked after me,
I was in prison and you came to visit me."*
MATTHEW 25:36 NIV

Listen. I hear the jailer's keys rattling." When Mary pulled her tattered skirt down to cover herself, her listless baby squealed a few weak cries of protest at the loss of warmth the thin material offered.

"Maybe Mistress Fry comes with more help." Hope lifted the veil of indifference from Gilda's face.

"A sane lady wouldn't return ta this stinkin' rat hole if'n a body had any choice in da matter." Nelda rolled over on the bare floor, but the other woman fastened her eyes on the slit in the heavy wooden door.

Prisoners who languished in nineteenth-century England prisons lived in miserable squalor. In the unheated, dank cells, people seldom enjoyed even a thin smattering of dirty straw on the cold floors when they tried to sleep. Almost no one possessed any sort of covering for the cold nights. Most prisoners wore inadequate clothing. Elizabeth Fry, a Quaker, was a quilt maker in nineteenth-century England when she learned of the dreadful conditions women prisoners suffered in the Newgate Prison in London, England. Warmed by fluffy quilts on her own comfortable bed, she couldn't ignore her horrified reaction when she learned of the wretched conditions incarcerated women endured. Some women even bore babies while imprisoned and had no blankets to wrap them in or clothing to warm them.

Not a woman content to sit and talk, Elizabeth took it upon herself to help. The attitude of the day hindered her efforts because people often considered poverty the justified lot of the poor and thought they shouldn't tamper with their status. Society considered the terrible prison conditions as part of the punishment for crimes. Authorities tried to discourage Elizabeth. Armed guards avoided entering the cells because they considered the prisoners extremely dangerous.

In spite of the warnings, Elizabeth enlisted the aid of women who were members of the Society of Friends. Together they began the challenging task of improving the living conditions of women in prison. The cries of children cold and sick from exposure, the numbed stares of mothers, helpless and without hope, drove the Quaker women to persevere in spite of the obstacles.

Elizabeth persuaded women to donate pile after pile of fabric scraps for the sewing classes she set up for imprisoned women. In spite of the stench of the prison, she and her volunteers taught the women how to turn the material scraps into clothing

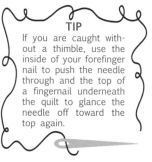

TIP
If you are caught without a thimble, use the inside of your forefinger nail to push the needle through and the top of a fingernail underneath the quilt to glance the needle off toward the top again.

and patchwork quilts to cover themselves in the cold. The gratitude of the women spurred the volunteers to increase their help and ignore any risk and discomfort.

When Elizabeth learned court judges often ordered women to travel by ship to penal colonies, she began to supply them with tea and other provisions for the long journey. She gave the women scraps for patchwork quilts that they made on the tedious voyage. Arriving at their destination without a penny, they could at least sell their quilts for a little money to improve their lot.

If we put our minds to it, God can give us creative ways to help others find a happier life. Elizabeth Fry not only offered help, she found a way to teach the women skills so they could help themselves in the future. Prisons still contain people in need of emotional soothing and comfort.

God's Pattern

By teaching others to sew and quilt, we pass on an
art form that allows the person to become productive.
Since God never becomes discouraged in offering us hope
and help, we can persist to offer the same to others.

Over and Over

That the generation to come might know them,
even the children which should be born; who
should arise and declare them to their children.
Psalm 78:6 kjv

Alice snuggled under the quilt on the four-poster bed in her grandmother's guest room. She loved bedtime when she visited her grandparents. After a bedtime story and before the good night kisses, she and Grandma played a game with the Flower Garden quilt. Alice pointed at a little piece of fabric and asked, "Whose dress was this?"

Grandma answered by saying things like, "The tiny pink flower material came from your mother's dress for her first piano recital. The yellow material was from Aunt Jan's dress for her first dance."

Alice knew the answers by heart and didn't need to ask anymore, but she never tired of hearing Grandma describe each event the many dresses had starred in. After Grandma heard her prayers and kissed her good night, Grandma turned on the dim light of the milk glass hurricane lamp in the corner of the room, and Alice could continue to look at her grandmother's Flower Garden quilt. She rubbed her fingers around each medallion and remembered the stories about when her mother and Aunt Jan were little girls, and when Grandma wore a blue-striped dress on her honeymoon to go to the theater for the first time ever.

Wrapped in the quilt and warmed by cozy memories of her heritage, Alice fell asleep planning for tomorrow.

Her tomorrows at Grandma's house were always fun. In the daytime the quilt served as a table for tea parties under the large oak tree, or the classroom where she taught her dolls their lessons, or the train of her gown when she played royal wedding.

TIP

When sewing many squares together on the machine, instead of cutting the thread at the end of each piece, begin sewing the next two squares together. Chain stitch in this manner until all the squares are finished. Cutting them apart later saves time.

Today the quilt is an important part of Alice's memories. She keeps it on her guest bed and can still recite the stories hidden in the pretty fabric of the quilt.

We become strong in God's principles the same way that Alice learned her heritage, by repetition. When we tell specific examples of when God blessed our family, we are preserving our children's spiritual heritage. The stories of the Lord's work in our lives improve our understanding of the kingdom of God. Because of the value of repetition, we read the same Bible over and over to grow and develop in understanding.

God's Pattern

Just as the repetition of a quilt pattern forms a pretty design for our blanket, repeatedly hearing examples of God's love for us establishes the message of God's goodness in our thinking. God commands us to teach the next generation His ways. "We will not hide them from their children, shewing to the generation to come the praises of the LORD, and his strength, and his wonderful works that he hath done" (Psalm 78:4 KJV).

Broken but Better

*The LORD is close to the brokenhearted and
saves those who are crushed in spirit.*
PSALM 34:18 NIV

Millie tried not to look in the mirror as she passed by it to turn on the shower, but her broken body had a magnetism about it that drew her attention. After a quick glance at herself, she averted her head from the mastectomy scars slashing their fresh, red streaks across her torso. The tears rolling down her cheeks in the shower felt hotter than the water.

"God, how do I go on from here? I feel so shattered, so broken. How do I live a whole life again in this disfigured body?" Millie felt powerless to overcome her feelings of uselessness.

The day loomed ahead like a blank canvas, only she couldn't find any colors to paint on it. At the thought of color, her friend's invitation to take a quilting class popped into her mind. Quilts radiated color. By the time she had dried and put on her clothes, she'd decided to do it. Maybe in class she'd think about something else besides her disfigurement.

Soon Millie lost herself in the delight of blending colors and pleasing designs from the rows of attractive fabric bolts. "Thanks," she said with a

TIP
Use a rotary cutter for a better finished product when piecing.

smile when her classmates complimented her choices. The process of cutting out pieces for the Star of the East pattern made her think of the cuts on her body. Here she was taking whole fabric, attractive as it lay all in one piece, and cutting it up into small diamonds, triangles, and squares. They didn't look like much by themselves; certainly not as attractive as the whole length of material had looked. However, when she pinned them together, they formed an elegant star. Pieces that looked useless by themselves formed a beautiful design, and together they looked far lovelier than any one of the fabrics alone. She learned to take care as she cut in order for her pieces to fit perfectly. She thanked God for taking care of her as the surgeon had used his skill on her body.

Millie wasted no time putting her finished quilt to use.

By day it decorated her bed; and in the evening she and her husband wrapped up in it when they watched TV. Neither did she waste any more time feeling useless. As a volunteer, she began to go to the hospitals and visit other mastectomy patients. She taught them exercises to prevent swelling and restore mobility to their arms, and she brought comfort born from shared pain.

God took the broken pieces of Millie's life and put them together into a new pattern and formed a useful life. Her grateful patients loved her. Millie came to appreciate the suffering of Jesus on the cross. He was broken for the benefit of all mankind.

◇◆◇◆◇◆◇◆◇

God's Pattern

"And when he had given thanks, he brake it, and said, Take, eat: this is my body, which is broken for you: this do in remembrance of me" (1 Corinthians 11:24 KJV). On a smaller scale, God takes our brokenness, as He took Christ's, and forms a beautiful new pattern for our lives.

Forever

I remember the days of old; I meditate on all thy works; I muse on the work of thy hands.

PSALM 143:5 KJV

"It's me, Grandma, Lucy. May I come in?" Lucy peered through the screen door where she could see her grandmother stitching on her latest quilt in the sunroom.

"Come in." Grandma motioned to Lucy with her hand. "What a sight you and baby Kelly make for my old eyes." Grandma reached an arm out to hug Lucy's waist. "Excuse me if I don't get up. I'm hurrying to get this quilt done before your brother Jason's wedding. Put the baby on the floor near my feet so I can watch her while I stitch."

"Why do you make so many quilts, Grandma?" Lucy watched as her grandmother pulled her needle in and out of her California Star quilt.

"I reckon you're too young to understand. I feel like I'm writing a little bit of history when I make a quilt. Some quilts tell stories about events in the history of our nation. Others are silent witnesses to the love of one person for another, like this quilt I'm making for your brother. I like to think I'm making Jason's life more comfortable with every patch I sew. Since a quilt takes so much time, it demonstrates my love."

"Wouldn't it be easier to buy a wedding gift?" Lucy asked.

"Easier, maybe, but it wouldn't represent my good wishes as well as this quilt

TIP

A small photo of the quilt maker photo-copied onto fabric and sewn to the back as part of a quilt label makes a nice memory jogger.

does. If I could stitch perpetual happiness, health, and joy into this comforter, I'd do it. Since I don't have that kind of supernatural power, I satisfy myself with sewing a pretty pattern and praying all the while I stitch for God to supply Jason's life with those blessings."

"I know you love me every morning when I make my bed and pull up the Wedding Ring quilt you made for me." Lucy leaned over and dropped a kiss on Grandma's forehead.

"Maybe my greatest motivation to quilt is striving for a certain amount of immortality. This quilt will still be warming Jason when I'm dead and gone. I hope it'll help him remember me."

"Oops." Lucy wiped Kelly's mouth when she spit up.

"I plan to make little Kelly a quilt next. Then if she never gets to know me as a grown-up, she'll know she once had a great-grandma who loved her because she'll own and handle my quilt."

"I'll always remember you, Grandma, with or without a quilt."

"I'm glad Jesus made a way for us to live forever in heaven and spend eternity with our loved ones who believe in Him, but when I make a quilt I like to think I'm making a memory jogger for the loved ones I leave behind. Maybe even a couple of generations after me will think a few warm thoughts about old Grandma Brown."

God supplied every human with immortality when we were born. Where we spend it depends on whether we accept Jesus as our Savior. The works of God's hand in our lives live on forever without deteriorating and rotting with age as our quilts will. Because of God's work, we have the choice of living forever with God where we will be reunited with our Christian loved ones.

God's Pattern

God designed our spirits to live forever.
Our search for immortality is fulfilled
when we make Jesus our Lord and Savior.

The Marvelous Middle

Though you have not seen him, you love him;
and even though you do not see him now,
you believe in him and are filled with
an inexpressible and glorious joy.

1 PETER 1:8 NIV

"Settle down," Laura said to her daughter, Candy. Laura twisted around in her chair at the quilt frame to give Candy a stern look. "Why don't you bring out the new puzzle for the children to put together while their mamas quilt?" She hoped the toy would buy some peace for the friends who had come to her house to quilt together.

The puzzle failed to hold the attention of the younger children, and the women's conversation leapfrogged over a steady stream of requests, complaints, or squabbles.

"Mothers have awesome mental skills to hang on to a thought through unlimited interruptions. Have we completed a sentence this morning without stopping in the middle?" Laura stuck her needle in the blue material in front of her and turned to unfasten Candy's overall straps in order for her to visit the bathroom. She plucked off a piece of Dacron polyfill that had migrated from the middle layer of the quilt to her daughter's rompers.

As lunch neared, the children's dispositions deteriorated.

TIP
Old blankets can be used for the middle of a quilt.

"They lost a piece to my new puzzle." Candy jogged her mother's elbow, her mouth turned down into a classic pout.

"It has to be around somewhere. Did you look on the floor?"

In spite of the interruptions, the friends continued and finished stitching a large section of the quilt before they stopped for lunch.

After lunch, the ladies seated themselves for one more short session. Hunter, the smallest boy, cuddled up with a quilt on the floor and fell asleep almost before putting his middle fingers in his mouth.

"Uh-oh." Laura laid down her needle and began to feel around the quilt. "I think I've found the puzzle piece."

Molly reached over and kneaded the quilt with one hand underneath and one on top. "You sure did. I can feel the little nibs on it."

"The trouble is that seven rows of stitches lie between the piece and the open edge. There's no way to get to it without ripping out a big chunk of this morning's work."

"It's a pretty thin piece of cardboard and tiny; could we pretend we never found it?"

Molly chuckled. "You know, like today's popular philosophy—if you don't see it, it doesn't matter."

Laura picked up her ripper and began to remove the little stitches. "It matters to Candy. She can't finish her puzzle without it. You make me think. What's hidden away in the middle of my personality you don't see and don't know about unless you happen to feel the lump it makes?"

Molly sat down beside Laura and began to help take out stitches. "Our spiritual life is like the middle of the quilt; it gives substance to us and warms our hearts but is invisible to the eye. I imagine God doesn't want lumps in the middle of our filling."

"Guess God is a little bit like the middle of a quilt, too. We can't see Him, but we know He's there by the warmth and blessings He wraps around us."

God's Pattern

Although we don't see God, we want Him in the middle of our lives providing for us. His presence and love give our lives meaning and allow us to rest like the baby rested on the quilt on the floor.

Eager Anticipation

Let us be glad and rejoice, and give honour to him:
for the marriage of the Lamb is come, and his wife
hath made herself ready. And to her was granted that
she should be arrayed in fine linen, clean and white:
for the fine linen is the righteousness of saints.
REVELATION 19:7–8 KJV

Bertha finished slicing her Sally Lund bread and laid the platter beside a bowl of golden butter. Giving the soup a final stir, she began ladling it into Mother's Wedgwood china bowls while her mother set out a plate of sugar cookies. "It's time for a recess to eat," she called to her extended family bent over the quilting frame.

The women stood and stretched their backs before moving toward the food. Too excited to eat, Bertha examined the morning's work on her wedding quilt. In between wreaths formed of red cherries and green leaves, muslin blocks held outlines of the handprints of her family, four generations. Under every hand, red thread spelled out the person's name and birth date. Bertha's sister had even made a square with her one-year-old daughter's handprint. Bertha stroked the flowers that formed a large heart in the middle of the quilt with her name and Mark's in the center.

"It's almost too beautiful to use."

"You'd better put this quilt on your guest bed and use it only for special occasions. It's too fancy to risk babies spitting up or diapers overflowing on it," Mother warned.

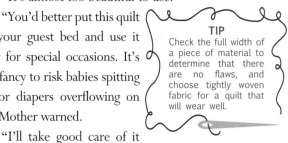

TIP
Check the full width of a piece of material to determine that there are no flaws, and choose tightly woven fabric for a quilt that will wear well.

"I'll take good care of it because the best part is having these hand outlines of my family. I love everyone so much." Bertha hugged her aunt who stood nearest to her. "Maybe Pennsylvania won't feel so far away when I look at this quilt on a Kansas homestead." A shadow passed over her face because her new life with Mark meant leaving her family behind.

"Is your wedding dress finished?" Bertha's cousin spoke up to fill in the awkward silence as the family thought about how far away Bertha would live.

"Nearly, but you can't see it until I walk down the aisle of the church." Bertha hugged herself and gave a shiver of anticipation.

"Not even of a swatch of the material?"

"Well, maybe a swatch." Bertha ran into a bedroom to bring out a sample of the airy white lawn fabric.

Making an extra fancy quilt to celebrate a wedding was a custom in the earlier days of our nation. Participation in the construction of the wedding quilt offered a way for family and friends to convey love and support for the bride and give tangible help to outfitting her first home.

Even today, a girl goes to great lengths to become a beautiful bride for her bridegroom. Brides spend large quantities of time, energy, and money on their preparations. Whatever sacrifices are involved seem small to the bride who is consumed with love for her bridegroom. In the picture of the marriage of Christ and His church, believers are symbolized as the bride of Christ. It is appropriate for us to lavish time and energy in preparing ourselves to greet our bridegroom with spiritual beauty. No effort is too great to make ourselves ready to please Christ.

God's Pattern

God supplies us with His righteousness in order that we may prepare ourselves to be a suitable bride for Christ.

Bearing Up

*Thy servant slew both the lion and the bear: and this
uncircumcised Philistine shall be as one of them, seeing
he hath defied the armies of the living God. David said
moreover, The LORD that delivered me out of the paw of
the lion, and out of the paw of the bear, he will deliver me
out of the hand of this Philistine. And Saul said unto David,
Go, and the LORD be with thee.*

1 SAMUEL 17:36–37 KJV

"It doesn't fit together right." Deanne threw the red and white squares onto Rene's lap. "I thought you said this is an easy quilt for a beginner."

"The Bear Paw pattern usually works well. It's all straight lines with no curves to throw things out of kilter." Rene studied the pieces.

" 'You can't go wrong' is what you said. Well, something's wrong. It looks weird when I sew the squares together." She stabbed the offending design with her finger. "The points of the toes are going every which way, and some are lots smaller than others." A giggle snuck up and overpowered her frustration. "The bear must have been a cripple."

"Did you check each block with a 'square up' ruler to be sure every one made a perfect square before you started the next piece?"

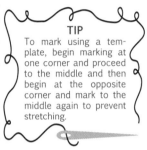

TIP

To mark using a template, begin marking at one corner and proceed to the middle and then begin at the opposite corner and mark to the middle again to prevent stretching.

"Check each block? The directions only said eight rows of ten blocks, so I made eighty blocks full speed ahead, but nothing works together. The edges are uneven along the sides when I try to sew this monstrosity into a complete quilt top."

Tugging at the material, Rene laid the pieces on a table. "I'm not sure what to do."

"I know exactly what to do with this quilt." Deanne picked up a nearby wastebasket and, holding it at the edge of the table, pushed the quilt pieces into it with an emphatic swipe of her arm. She slammed her sewing machine back into its case and marched into the kitchen. In a moment she returned and slapped a cookbook in front of Rene, who sat in her chair, trying to keep her mouth from gaping open.

"Here's something I understand. I follow the cookbook recipe instructions, and I have a lovely, light cake or creamy pudding for my efforts. I'll leave the quilting to you and feed you while you do it."

Although Deanne refused to try the Bear Paw pattern again, she did stick with learning to quilt in spite of her early frustrations. As she grew in knowledge of what the craft required, she developed more patience and came to appreciate God's faithfulness to her in spite of the imperfections of her character. Many times when she'd catch herself not fitting into God's plan, she'd think of the Bear Paw quilt and adopt a more cooperative attitude.

God's Pattern

The purpose of His design for us is to form a beautiful design for the kingdom of God. Frustration grates our soul, but we can allow God to use it to refine our character. Fitting into His pattern brings us the skill of discerning good in life's lows as well as the highs.

Watch Out

We are confident, I say, and willing rather to be absent from the body, and to be present with the Lord.
2 Corinthians 5:8 KJV

Grandmother Konane reached a hand out from under the sheet and touched her granddaughter. "The family quilts. . ." Her waning strength reduced her voice to a whisper. "Guard them from prying eyes. Treasure them. They record the love, feelings, and events of our ancestors. Check every week for mildew and be vigilant against the pests that have destroyed so many Hawaiian quilts."

She struggled to raise her shoulders from the bed. "Look in the cedar chest for my Royal Flag quilt. Take out the one where all the red and blue strips run up and down. I made it, and my *mana* rests in that quilt. . . ." Too weak to continue, her voice trailed off.

"Rest, Grandmother. I'll find it and bring it to your bedroom, and you can tell me if I've located the quilt your spirit rests in." Lani squeezed her grandmother's hand before walking through the door to an anteroom.

When the maid waiting for instructions saw how the tears blurred Lani's vision, she helped lift the quilts from the chest.

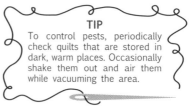

TIP
To control pests, periodically check quilts that are stored in dark, warm places. Occasionally shake them out and air them while vacuuming the area.

Lani stood by the light from the window and read the date Grandmother had embroidered on the back of the two-color Royal Hawaiian Flag quilt.

"When Grandmother made this in 1879, she was fifty years old," Lani told the maid who helped her unfold the quilt. Lani looked out over the clear blue Malala Bay from her Honolulu home. "What a lot of Hawaiian history she has seen. She refused to make a Hawaiian Flag quilt after the annexation to the United States in 1898. I didn't know she had made so many quilts. I seldom saw Grandmother's Hawaiian quilts displayed."

Carrying the quilt, Lani returned to her grandmother's bedside and found her asleep. Pulling up a chair, she waited to see if she had found the right comforter. Since it felt hot on her lap, she laid it on a nearby table. In Hawaii, quilts were for artistic expression, not warmth.

Grandmother smiled when she opened her eyes and saw Lani with the quilt. "My spirit rests here," she said, pointing to the red and blue flag. "Burn it when I die."

The strength of her grip surprised Lani. "I don't want you to die."

"Hush, child, I know my days are few. Burn the quilt when my last breath leaves."

"But it's so beautiful, and we want something to remember you by."

"I've made other quilts and lots of Royal Hawaiian Flag quilts. This one you are to burn to protect my mana. Will you carry out my wishes, or must I ask another?"

"Yes, Grandmother." Now Lani's voice sounded weaker than her grandmother's.

How grateful we are that our spirit doesn't linger around the earth after we die, haunting places or things. Instead, those of us who have received Jesus into our lives will live in the presence of God for all eternity.

Because Hawaiians carefully guarded their quilt patterns, not wanting anyone to copy them, Hawaiian quilts were not often displayed. Today's quilter is eager to share patterns and expertise with others.

God's Pattern

Our spirit lives forever. God made a plan that provides for our spirit to live eternally with God. God wants us to share the pattern He designed for eternal life with others.

Patience

*For ye have need of patience, that, after ye have
done the will of God, ye might receive the promise.*
Hebrews 10:36 kjv

*And let us not be weary in well doing:
for in due season we shall reap, if we faint not.*
Galatians 6:9 kjv

W hat's this?" Ben opened the next box on the attic
shelf.

"A quilt I started," Clara answered. "I never finished it
because it was taking so long."

"You're a fine one to talk. You're always fussing at me
because I didn't finish something. You never did get off my
back about the unfinished bird feeder."

"I'd forgotten how pretty the Fan pattern is." Clara
ignored her son, pulled the half-finished coverlet out of the
box, and held it up to the faint attic light.

"Mother, you're always saying, 'Finish what you

start.' " Ben enjoyed feeling like he had the upper hand and continued to tease his mother.

"Maybe I *will* finish this. I like how I shaded the blues from light to dark. Let's take it down and look at it in good light. I think I stopped when I started doing the PTA treasurer's job.

"Remember my friend Marge? She and I made quilts together. She paid someone to quilt hers after she finished piecing the top. I never finished the top. Some people like the piecing best and some people like the quilting part."

TIP
Quilting with someone makes the time go faster.

"The man who owns the department store where I work likes to piece quilts on a machine." Ben carried the quilt down the attic ladder. "He has no patience for quilting and always hires it out."

Quilting by machine has changed the time required to make a quilt. By hand, the process takes time. Any task or hobby that requires a long time from start to finish is profitable for character development. When a person learns to delay gratification for a better reward in the end, he or she develops patience. Patience helps us when we find ourselves in situations that are beyond our control.

Sometimes we are not able to find answers for our circumstances in a hurry. Certainly in rearing children, we can't hasten their maturing. As children grow, they try our patience. Qualities important to adult living don't spring into existence overnight. When we find ourselves powerless in the face of adversities, we will press through to reap the fruit of our efforts if we have learned not to faint at difficulties. First comes the patience and then the promise.

God's Pattern

God's promises are steadfast. He gives the strength to hold on to them even when we feel weary and faint.

Bleeding

*But one of the soldiers with a spear pierced his side, and
forthwith came there out blood and water.*

John 19:34 kjv

"O uch." The thin, sharp needle penetrated Cher's finger
so deeply it left a scarlet trail as she pulled her hand
out from underneath the quilt. Before she realized how
much she was bleeding, bright drops splattered on her
pineapple appliquéd square.

Recovery from the jab did not concern Cher nearly as
much as the stains on her quilt. "Can you get these stains
out, Mr. Barr?" Cher asked the dry cleaner where she took
her quilt, hoping for help.

"That depends. It looks like you've already worked on
them. What did you try?"

"First I used cold water. When those stubborn places
on the pineapple shapes didn't come out"—Cher pointed
to the serrated points of the golden fabric—"I tried a

commercial stain remover. Next, I tried hair spray. My neighbor said that always works, but it didn't."

The man behind the counter sighed as he shook his head. "No, it often sets a stain. Did you ever let hot water touch it?"

"Well, maybe a little when I washed out the hair spray." A sinking feeling dropped into Cher's middle when she saw Mr. Barr frown and stroke the remaining lock of hair he plastered across the top of his head.

"If you've put hot water on bloodstains, we probably can't remove them completely."

"I've spent hours and days, no, weeks on this quilt," Cher wailed. "It's a gift for my sister's twenty-fifth wedding anniversary." She struggled to bring her voice back to a normal level. "Do something."

"We can try bleach on the white background, but bleach will affect the printed fabric. It often fades colors." Mr. Barr tugged his hair until it fell to the side, leaving his shiny head bare.

Afraid Mr. Barr was right and her quilt would never again look as good as new, Cher did not wait to see the result. She stopped at the store on the way home and bought supplies to begin another quilt right away.

The clerk was adamant that she should use a size nine

needle when doing the appliqué and switch to a size ten needle when she began quilting. She winced when she laid out her needles, realizing what had caused her to ruin her project. Not owning the right sizes, she had substituted a size seven needle. In her struggle to push the too large needle through all the layers, she had resorted to force and stabbed herself hard.

Fretting over her deadline, she changed the design of her pineapples, giving them smooth sides instead of ser-

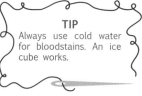

TIP
Always use cold water for bloodstains. An ice cube works.

rated and reduced their number in order to minimize the time required to cut and stitch a new top. "Sis is worth my best; I'll do whatever it takes to get a pretty quilt to her by her anniversary."

When Jesus shed His blood on the cross, He didn't take shortcuts but gave His best—to give us the gift of eternal life. We could not earn it even if we smoothed the sides of our lives and stitched the pieces with all our might. The blood and water which flowed when the Roman soldier pierced His side brought horror and grief to the bystanders, but it brought a witness to His followers throughout the centuries that Jesus had secured life for them at the sacrifice of His blood.

God's Pattern

His blood shed on the cross made complete
atonement for our sin. By accepting His sacrifice,
we attain salvation. The stains of our life are removed.

You're Somebody

To the praise of the glory of his grace,
wherein he hath made us accepted in the beloved.
Ephesians 1:6 kjv

I'm sorry I came here. My room is too small, and I'm lonely. I don't know anybody who lives here," Gladys complained to her visitor, Roma, about the nursing home where she had lived for only two weeks.

"Next time I come, I'll bring you lots of company. Wouldn't it be fun to see the Sunday school class you used to teach?" Since Roma had taken over the class, she faithfully stayed in touch with Gladys, the retired church secretary.

"Can't have them in this tiny place." Gladys waved her arm, indicating her room. "Anyway, they've grown up a lot since I taught them. They won't want to bother with an old lady like me."

The next day, during Roma's ninth-grade Sunday

school class, she told the girls how hard it is for some older people to adjust to new surroundings. The girls jumped at Roma's idea of making and taking a lap quilt to Gladys.

Each girl embroidered her name on a square of material she brought from home. Roma embroidered "With love from your Sunday school class" on the center square and sewed the squares together. The girls had a quilt-tying party at Roma's house and planned a celebration to present the gift.

Ten girls arrived early at the nursing home to decorate the lounge with crepe paper and banners, broadcasting their love for Gladys. They set out punch and cookies. Meanwhile, the staff brought many of the other residents into the lounge. Then Roma went to Gladys's room, fluffed her gray hair into a pretty frame around her face, settled her into a wheelchair, and rolled her into the lounge.

TIP
By signing one's name in pencil and then embroidering over it, not only is the name recorded but a sample of the person's handwriting is preserved.

"Surprise!" the girls shouted. For a moment, Roma wondered if she'd used bad judgment, surprising an eighty-six-year-old woman; but, after a stunned look, a wide smile stretched Gladys's thin lips and pumped bright color into her cheeks.

"We made you a present." The tallest girl put the puffy package on Gladys's lap. Gladys's smile competed with tears when she saw what the girls had made for her. As the other residents crowded around to admire the lap quilt, the smile won.

The girls arranged themselves on the steps in the lobby and sang hymns and choruses, urged on by the applause and appreciation of their audience. Soon old, wavering voices joined young vibrant ones to lift praises to God.

While the residents enjoyed the refreshments, Gladys kept stroking the quilt and saying, "I can't believe you did this."

When she mailed a thank-you note to the class, the nursing home staff enclosed a note.

You girls did not realize you were giving your former Sunday school teacher a gift more important than the lap quilt which warms her body as she sits in her wheelchair. The attention you gave increased her importance in the eyes of the other residents and helped her feel accepted in our little community.

God understands our need for acceptance and will

provide it at the right time. Times of loneliness or times of experiencing rejection may also bring about the design of God for our lives. We can allow our need for acceptance to drive us closer to God and deepen our understanding of His favor.

God's Pattern

When the rejection or neglect of people grieves us,
we can cover ourselves with the acceptance of God
and grow warm in His presence. Human companionship
is attracted to us as our demeanor grows cheerful
from delighting in Him.

God's Stitchery

*I will praise thee; for I am fearfully and
wonderfully made: marvellous are thy works.*
PSALM 139:14 KJV

"What's this?" Joanne pointed to the blue lines that
meandered around Polly's quilt.

"They're washable marks to guide my quilting stitches."
Polly showed Joanne a section where she had already
stitched the lines with white thread on the white muslin.

"But it doesn't have any design or consistent pattern.
It just wanders around. Sorta reminds me of the lines my
kindergartner scribbles all over her paper before she fills
them in with her crayons."

"Maybe it's a notch above a kindergarten scribble."
Polly decided not to take offense. "You'll notice none of
the lines cross over each other. It's called Stepple quilting.
I know it seems aimless, but it really holds the layers
of material together well, and it serves the purpose of

keeping the fabric flat."

"I have to admit the places you have already finished look nice once you got rid of the blue line. Is the line hard to take out? It looks like ink."

"It disappears the minute I put cold water on it. Hot water is a no-no. It sets the color instead of making it vanish."

Sometimes we feel as if the pattern of our lives has become aimless and without color. We don't understand

TIP
To remove the lines made with a water-soluble pencil, spray with a mist bottle filled with cold water.

the design that our circumstances are drawing. We may feel we have lost our purpose. We endure these stages better if we remember God is the Master quilter of our lives. He began with a marvelous plan, and He knows the finest way to achieve it. He knows the right places to establish a flatness and lack of color to provide a pleasing contrast to the patterns where He stitches vivid events and triumphs into our lives. The blue marker, which disappears when touched by cold water, reminds us that the ugly marks sin writes on our souls disappear with the touch of God's forgiveness. When we repent from bad choices and attitudes, God is faithful to cleanse us from the stain of sin.

God's Pattern

When God formed us, He knew His wonderful plan for our lives. Even when we have messed up His plan, He continues to work His design in us and provide the stitches to hold us together.

The Scarlet Quilt

*And be ye kind one to another, tenderhearted,
forgiving one another, even as God for
Christ's sake hath forgiven you.*
EPHESIANS 4:32 KJV

"Trish, have you met Mona?" Sandy reached out to stop her friend Trish, who was passing down the church aisle after the service. "Mona's been coming to our church for about a month now."

Trish gave the young woman a sideways hug. Mona's advanced pregnancy made any other kind impossible. "When's the baby due?"

"December second."

Mona looked at the floor, and Trish gave Sandy a questioning look.

"Maybe one of your teenagers could help Mona after school when the baby is born," Sandy suggested.

"Sure, do you have other children?" Trish asked.

"No."

Trish felt Sandy's knuckles jab her in the back, and Trish decided she'd better stop with the questions. "What's going on?" she asked when Mona had moved down the aisle. "What's with the kidney punch?"

"The daddy of Mona's baby disappeared when he learned she was pregnant. They never married. I guess after that, the Lord reminded Mona of her childhood roots in the church."

"She's brave to come back. I hope people will hold their tongues and show kindness."

Indeed, the church ladies outdid themselves showing kindness. Although the news of Mona's situation traveled fast, the ladies' responses reflected the character of Jesus. Instead of asking embarrassing questions about where Daddy was, the congregation asked what she needed. The women decided that the innocent child, conceived in lust, would receive love and welcome in God's church family.

Trish took a special interest in the situation. "Do you notice how embarrassed Mona seems?" Trish asked Sandy. "She has a hard time lifting her eyes to meet anyone's gaze when we talk to her. How can we make her feel accepted? We may not have had our babies out of wedlock, but we've all made mistakes we regret and needed God's forgiveness."

The women's prayer circle decided to host a baby shower and to make a quilt for the event. Using baby colors, each woman pieced a block about the love of God. In order to finish the blanket before the shower, they tied it together with yarn instead of quilting it.

The attendance of dozens of women pleased the hostesses and overwhelmed Mona. With each gift she unwrapped, her eyes grew larger. As the stack of gifts grew, Trish said, "We're determined to make your li'l punkin the best outfitted kid in the church."

TIP
When vacuuming a quilt to remove dust, make a fiberglass screen and cover the rough edges with tape. By placing the screen over the quilt you will not suck the fabric into the vacuum.

With her eyes studying her shoes, Mona stammered her thanks. Everyone fell silent to watch her open the last gift, the quilt. "Do you really love me this much?" Mona whispered as she lifted the quilt from its tissue-paper cocoon. When Mona stood to show everyone the quilt, she lifted her head and looked around the room. "How can you love me enough to do all this when I'm. . .I'm. . .I've made a lot of mistakes?" Her chin quivered.

"Hey, we all needed the death of Jesus on the cross to cover our mistakes." Sandy took Mona's hand. "Since God's forgiveness means He's forgotten the mistake, we chose not to dwell on it also."

"How many people fit into the hospital waiting room?" Trish asked. "We all want to come dance with the angels when the baby is born."

"Hear that, li'l punkin? You have a welcome committee waiting." Mona lifted her head and looked from face to face. She didn't know the broad smiles were as much for her ability to look them in the eye as for her words.

The women's tender kindness gave Mona a glimpse of God's grace, which helped her accept His forgiveness. After the gift of the quilt, she held her head up and faced the challenges of her life, confident that God did not reject her because of her sin but, rather, had provided a way to erase it.

God's Pattern

When we offer kindness and forgiveness for others in times of failure, we demonstrate God's mercy. We all require the depths of His grace for our daily living.

Dog Begone

Good-bye." Shannon stood in the doorway and waved as her quilt guild walked down the driveway to their cars. "I'll attach the entry information to each quilt before I bring them to the hotel for the exhibit."

Her three hounds bounded into the house while she held the door open.

"Don't let those dogs in the house while you have our quilts spread out over your floor." Winona slammed her car door and marched back up the walk and into the front door. "Dogs are as bad as moths for quilts. I can't believe you let those dogs in, Shannon." She took Shannon's arm and pulled her toward the family room where the women had left their quilts spread out over the floor. "If I'd known you had dogs, three no less, I'd have never left my quilt here."

She paused at the doorway, her mouth dropping open. There the three hounds were stepping carefully between the quilts, picking the narrow inches in between the comforters to put their feet. Not a single paw step fell on the quilts.

When Bongo, the largest hound, reached the recliner, he jumped up and began to curl around and around until he was satisfied with his position and dropped down with a sigh. The other two hounds eased their way toward the sofa on the far wall. Winona held her breath while Bingo sidled past her quilt. He leaped heavily onto a pillow and looked back at Winona with mournful eyes that seemed aggrieved at her distrust of him.

"Well, I never. . ." Winona stopped, unable to hide her surprise. "Every dog I know makes a beeline for a quilt as if the whole purpose of making one is to furnish the pooch with a soft nap."

Shannon laughed and took Winona's hand off her arm where it was leaving a mark from her tense grip. "Not my bassets. You saw them take great pains not to step on them. Avoiding ten big quilts to get to the couch took some doing."

"Maybe they're careful because we're looking. I'll bet if we went into the living room and sneaked back in a few minutes, they'd all have picked out the softest ones for a nap."

"I don't know why, but they seem to know the quilts are off-limits for them. Wish they felt the same way about the furniture." Shannon gave a wry smile.

For some mysterious reason, Shannon's dogs respected the work of the quilters. Good manners taught at a young age help us learn to show consideration to others and their property. Respecting others even when they annoy us comes easier when we recognize everyone is the creation of God. When we defer to others, we take care not to step on their feelings or hurt them.

TIP
Many judges disqualify a quilt for a show if they find cat or dog hair on it!

Honoring God leads us to live carefully around the world of His creation, our earth. A little extra thought helps us preserve the things of nature He created for us to enjoy. Most important, we hold God in the highest esteem, for He alone is holy. He is worthy of our awe and reverence.

God's Pattern

As the people in biblical days removed their
shoes to demonstrate their reverence,
our adoration of God causes us to desire to
remove any steps that would not honor our God.

The Quarrel

*[God] has given us new birth. . .
into an inheritance that can never perish,
spoil or fade. . .kept in heaven for you.*
1 Peter 1:3–4 niv

"I suppose you want Mother's wedding album, too." Gina didn't try to hide the sarcasm in her voice as she pulled the book off the shelf and held it over a packing box.

"I am the oldest; and since I host all the family gatherings, it makes sense for me to keep it where people will have the most opportunity to see it." Cora reached for the leather volume.

Gina bit her tongue against the sharp words pounding across her mind. Beginning the day their mother died, the sisters had argued over the distribution of her possessions.

By the time the daughters began to clean out the attic, hostility prickled as badly as the heat in the air. When Gina opened a black plastic garbage bag, she swallowed a gasp of delight. It was full of lovely fabric scraps. *Perfect for my quilting,* she thought and tucked it over in a corner, planning to carry it down the steps and out to her car unnoticed later.

However, her plan crumbled when she came across two more garbage bags of scraps. *Three bags of scraps are too many to sneak out of the attic,* she thought. She turned when she heard Cora chortle behind her.

There her sister was, leaning over two more garbage bags piled to the top with leftover pieces of material from some of their mother's many projects. "Perfect. I can make my kids quilts from these."

"You'll never do it. You just talk about quilting," Gina protested. "I'll really use them. I should get the bags."

"Look, you're standing by two bags and there's another one over in the corner." Cora gestured toward the bag Gina had thought she'd hidden. "We'll split them."

"I quilt twice as much as you." Gina didn't try to keep her voice down.

"Now that all the kids are in school, I'm going to do more."

"Where are you?" At the call of their husbands arriving to take them to dinner, the sisters stopped arguing and clambered down to wash up.

The next morning when the sisters climbed to the

attic, Cora's voice shrilled with rage. "Where are the fabric scraps?"

Gina didn't answer.

"Did you take them? You did. I can tell by your face. You took them all. You didn't even leave me one."

TIP
A good way to store inherited quilts is to roll them on a long fabric-covered tube.

Gina backed down the stairs at the sight of her sister's face.

Angry words and unleashed hostility rang through the house, ending with both sisters screeching out of the driveway in their cars. The girls haven't spoken to each other since. A relationship of a lifetime cut to shreds because of five garbage bags of scraps. The inheritance of the sisters drove a wedge and spoiled their peace.

Parents who don't want their children quarreling over their possessions after they die are wise to write wills to eliminate arguing. Better yet, parents should try to raise their children to value relationships over possessions. Our wise heavenly Father has prepared a better inheritance for us than any human parent can provide. It doesn't fade like fabric scraps will surely do. It lasts forever, and its value is beyond measure.

God's Pattern

God's will is for us to inherit eternal life and understand that which comes later is better than that which comes first. This life pales in comparison to life everlasting.

Did You Know?

Yea, the darkness hideth not from thee;
but the night shineth as the day:
the darkness and the light are both alike to thee.
PSALM 139:12 KJV

The Woods family always referred to the summer
of Kenny's illness as the dark summer. While the
frequently cloudy days cast gloom over the landscape of
their home, the gray atmosphere that shrouded the inside
of the Woodses' home challenged even the electric lights to
dispel it. Three-year-old Kenny suffered from a dangerous
disease.

Billy and his brother Brian never let on to their friends,
but they welcomed the rainy days when they worked on their
quilts while their mother stitched hers. Right after school
closed in June, Mother had helped them cut the diamond
and square shapes for their Tumbling Block pattern. When
the boys arranged the pieces correctly, contrasting the light
squares with the dark diamonds, the shapes looked like

real, three-dimensional blocks.

As the summer passed, the boys took turns sharing jokes with their little brother, who lay in a bed while they worked on their quilts. Kenny enjoyed the companionship, and his big brothers liked the sense of accomplishment they gained from watching their Tumbling Block project grow. The reward of watching Kenny enjoy the blocks on their quilt when he was too sick to play with real blocks kept them diligently returning to their stitching all summer long. Mom said that someday the treatments would make Kenny strong enough to build a block tower with real blocks. In the meantime he liked to trace his finger around the block outlines and try to figure out how flat material could look like real cubes.

Whenever a friend rang the doorbell, Billy and Brian stuffed their quilts under a chair before running to answer it. One day their next-door neighbor didn't do the courtesy of ringing the

TIP

A color wheel, often available in paint stores, helps determine which colors provide the most light and dark contrast.

bell. Tom marched unannounced into the house to find the boys with their quilts in their laps. Billy and Brian froze, their needles in their hands. Mrs. Woods interrupted Tom's derisive whoop before he could follow it up with scornful words.

"Tom, if you behave yourself, you can join the boys. They're training to be president of the United States."

All three boys stared at Mrs. Woods in disbelief.

"When Dwight D. Eisenhower and Calvin Coolidge were boys, probably around the same age as you fellows, they helped their mothers make quilts. Dwight Eisenhower made a Tumbling Block quilt just like the ones Billy and Brian are working on, and Calvin Coolidge made a Baby Block quilt, which is the same pattern only using pastel colors suitable for babies."

"What's that got to do with being president?" Tom managed to stop gaping and ask.

"They learned not to succumb to peer pressure by doing something considered unusual for boys. They learned to examine their actions for value instead of making their decisions for appearances. By learning to stand alone they became men who were willing to stick by their principles when they were grown. A very important quality for a president, don't you think?"

"Yes, ma'am." Tom stood, feeling awkward.

"Tell you what. You can help entertain Kenny by telling him about your day. A little distraction brightens his outlook after his treatments."

"Kinda like our bright quilts," Billy said. "The contrast

of the dark material lying next to the light material makes the cubes look so real."

"The boys and I will put everything away while you talk. We were nearly ready to stop for pizza. Would you like to have lunch with us?"

"Yes, ma'am." This time Tom's voice sounded pleased.

Learning new skills stretches our abilities and expands our horizons. A willingness to risk the label of being different opens us up to explore new talents and more profitable attitudes. In the New Testament, Peter broke from the accepted path when he took the good news of the gospel to the Gentiles. Millions of Christians are thankful he found the courage to break tradition and preach to non-Jewish people.

◇◇◇◇◇◇◇

God's Pattern
Remain flexible and listen for God's direction.
"For thou wilt light my candle: the LORD my God will enlighten my darkness" (Psalm 18:28 KJV).

Happy Faces

*Happy is he that hath the God of Jacob for his help, whose
hope is in the LORD his God.*
PSALM 146:5 KJV

Sally bit her lip as she concentrated on her crayon picture.
Seated next to her, Mary Jo chewed on a corner of her
Brownie uniform handkerchief. Unusual quiet reigned as
the entire Brownie troop plied their fabric crayons to their
muslin squares.

"I'll draw a rainbow if you'll make a flower under it,"
Sally told Mary Jo. "Fern likes rainbows."

"I'm drawing a sun with my flowers," another Brownie
Scout piped up.

"I'm making lots of hearts so Fern will know we love
her. When can Fern come back to our Brownie meeting?"
Mary Jo asked.

"Probably not for several months. Both she and her
brother have a lot of injuries from the accident. Getting

well will take time," the troop leader said.

"I'm ready to start on her brother's quilt. What can we draw for Grady's quilt?" Mary Jo asked.

"Boys don't want lots of hearts and flowers." Sally shared her wisdom learned from a large family of brothers. "They like smiley faces, especially if they feel sick."

TIP
A vinegar rinse helps set colors applied to fabric. Place waxed paper over a crayon drawing on a fabric and iron to set the color.

"Will Grady throw up on our quilt?" Mary Jo looked up with alarm in her eyes.

"He just broke bones," Sally said. "He didn't break his stomach."

After the girls had drawn their pictures, the troop leader took the squares home and sewed them together. The next week at the Brownie meeting, the girls tied the layers together with bright-colored yarn. The mothers drove the troop to the hospital the next day to present their gifts.

The girls found Grady sound asleep from his pain medication. When Sally and Mary Jo spread the cover over his quiet form, tears slid down his mother's cheeks. The deep creases on the single woman's face betrayed the strain she felt from caring for two injured children.

Next everyone visited Fern. Her wide-awake eyes

sparkled with delight over the quilt, and her mother, Ms. Trevor, helped the troop leader hang it on the wall at the end of the bed where she could see it.

"I've felt so alone." Ms. Trevor reached out her arms and hugged as many girls as she could gather in. "I'll always think of brown as the color of hope because you sweet Brownies came with these gifts of love. Your love has renewed my hope in God."

Our hope for solutions to illness, finances, relationship difficulties, or any type of trouble rests in God. The same faithfulness God showed Jacob in long-ago Bible days is available to us today, and we do count ourselves happy because He stands ready to help us.

God's Pattern

The God of today continues the pattern
of the faithful God of the Old Testament.
He offers hope for every situation.

Make New Friends

A man that hath friends must shew himself friendly:
and there is a friend that sticketh closer than a brother.
PROVERBS 18:24 KJV

Two are better than one; because they
have a good reward for their labour.
ECCLESIASTES 4:9 KJV

She sat alone on the Florida beach and watched the waves roll toward her bare feet. Children romped far to the right, and the couple on her left slept on a towel.

"This is ridiculous," Megan informed a sand fiddler who scurried past her toes. "I like the beach. I love the cozy feeling of this town. I'm crazy about my new house. And I don't miss the cad I left behind in Mississippi. But I'm so lonely I could cry." And she did, allowing quiet sobs to escape while she sat with her knees drawn up to her chin in case someone passed by and she needed to hide her face.

"That does it. Time to take some steps when I bawl on

the beach—my best therapy location." Her eyes traveled unseeing over the newspaper she had brought with her until an ad caught her attention. "That's the answer," Megan said and stuffed her towel, sunscreen, and newspaper into her beach bag. Picking up her chair, she trudged over the sand toward the car. Her trudge became a run when she left the moist sand near the water and the hot ground scorched her feet.

Back home, she dialed the number in the paper while her chicken TV dinner heated in the microwave.

Long after the bell announced her dinner was ready, she was still enjoying an animated conversation with the president of the local quilt guild. "I'll be there, seven o'clock tomorrow night at the library. See you then."

Megan was surprised how quickly she felt comfortable with the guild ladies. Bringing her quilt paved the way for easy conversation. Sharing a hobby in common with the women made her feel friendly and comfortable. Noticing one of the women didn't wear a wedding ring, she shifted her chair nearby, thinking if the woman was also single she might have a free evening. To Megan's delight the lady accepted her

> **TIP**
> Check with the library, YWCA, or quilting supply stores to find local quilting guilds.

invitation for dinner the following week.

In the weeks and months that followed, the quilt guild became the focus of Megan's social life. Her involvement branched out to include other activities with the ladies.

"I don't know what I would have done when I moved here if it wasn't for this guild," she reported one night. "When my husband left me to marry another woman, I thought I had lost forever the advantages of the Bible verse which says two are better than one. But you all make me forget I'm one. I'm no longer lonely."

One of the blessings that accompanies a hobby is the way it opens opportunities for friendships with people one might never have known otherwise. When we are pursuing an area of mutual interest, it helps us overcome shyness. Showing ourselves friendly becomes easier.

God's Pattern

Friends provide strength to one another.
Shared companionship brightens life.
God's pattern is to look for ways to
include people in our activities and
to avoid being exclusive.

God's Pattern

Direct my footsteps according to your word;
let no sin rule over me.
PSALM 119:133 NIV

Linda's face twisted with pain when she wrapped in tissue paper the baby blanket her grandmother had knit. "Why, Lord?" Linda laid the blanket on top of the crib sheets in the cardboard carton. The pink and blue yarn showed through the thin paper. Not knowing the sex of the baby, Grandma had used both colors for her gift.

"It could have been all blue, Grandma," Linda whispered. "James was a boy." She stopped to wipe her eyes, almost surprised they could produce any more tears. She had done little else but cry since the miscarriage a month ago. Unable to bear any more regrets, she fled the nursery and ran down the stairs. Without thinking, she punched the phone's automatic dial button for her mother.

"I can't do it." Linda's words were garbled by her sobs.

"Everyone says I need to pack all the baby stuff away and get on with living. I tried, but I can't stand it."

In record time Linda's mother wheeled her car into the driveway and let the screen door bang behind her as she entered the house.

"You don't need to do this all by yourself. I'll help you." With their arms wrapped around one another's waists, they climbed up the stairs and entered the silent nursery.

"Do I need to paint over the rocking horse paper border Joel and I hung? Is that part of putting it all behind me?"

"Of course not. You'll have another baby someday, but you don't want dusty clothes so we'll store these things in the attic in the meantime."

"How do I know I'll ever have another baby? Nothing makes any sense." Linda sank into the rocking chair. She leaned forward to pull the brown teddy bear from behind her back and threw it across the room. "My life is out of control. There's no reason for anything."

"Life feels like that sometimes," Mom said. "I have an idea of what will help. There's a new quilting class starting at the fabric shop in the mall. Nothing like making a quilt to give you a sense of purpose and control."

Desperate for distraction, Linda took the class. She concentrated on cutting the sizes accurately. Planning for the progression of colors from light to dark in her Log Cabin quilt seemed to restore her sense of order. To ensure an attractive overall appearance, she had to design and plan ahead. As she decided which colors to use for her short and long strips, she thought about God, who knew ahead when dark patches would cloud her world. If she could use her dark strips to the best advantage in a small thing like a quilt, she knew God would use the dark places in her life to make a pleasing pattern even if she couldn't see it or understand it yet.

Linda began to trust Him as the Perfect Designer even if she never did understand the "whys" of her experience. "When life feels out of control to me, God is still there," she reassured herself. As she sewed, she found she could pray again. "Order my steps, Lord. Don't let my heartache overpower my love for You."

Each added strip built a pretty blend of colors that created an overall pattern beyond the individual design of each block. Linda was delighted with the results. As her satisfaction grew, she found her joy returning. While she began to enjoy the process of quilting, she began to delight once again in her God and trust Him with her hopes and disappointments.

God's Pattern

If we keep our heart focused on the goodness of God,
the Master planner, we can find hope and
encouragement to weather our storms.

Design for Wholeness

*We who are strong ought to bear with the
failings of the weak and not to please ourselves.*
Romans 15:1 niv

Shasta lay speechless on her hospital bed. All she could do was look in gratitude at her friends gathered at her bedside. The group could not have thought of a better gift for her. Shasta spread the quilt top out on the sheet.

"It's perfect," Shasta stammered, and then the words began to tumble. "This will be better therapy for me than the chemo the doctor insists I must take."

"We've basted the twelve blocks to the batting and backing so it's all ready for you to quilt. We hope the project will fill time for you while you wait on your treatments and twiddle your thumbs in doctors' offices," Diane said.

"And here I was worrying about wasting time and feeling bored for these long weeks ahead. You've given me a great way to distract myself from my illness and stop worrying about my health. Tell me who made which block?" she asked and then answered herself. "I see you each signed them."

Shasta listened with delight as the women chattered about the squares, telling why they had selected the various patterns and how the colors all seemed to fit together.

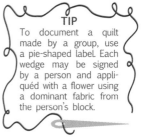

TIP

To document a quilt made by a group, use a pie-shaped label. Each wedge may be signed by a person and appliquéd with a flower using a dominant fabric from the person's block.

"This package holds the rest of the present." A portable quilting hoop, a package of needles, a thimble, and a spool of thread tumbled out of Carrie's sack onto the bed.

"Don't forget this." Diane held up a large, hand-quilted tote bag. "You can use it to carry everything back and forth to the hospital for chemotherapy."

"Our quilt will become my greatest treasure. Line up for hugs." She let go of Carrie to ask, "How did all twelve of you get in here? Isn't it against the rules?"

"We bribed the head nurse. She quilts, and said our gift was better than medicine. It didn't hurt to leave her a package of needles. Just don't let her use them on you."

"Bet those thin quilting needles would feel better than the ones she uses." Shasta rolled her eyes.

Shasta faithfully carried her quilting project to her daily treatments. To her surprise, she never tired too much to quilt a little, helping to pass the time faster. Even at home, she quilted although she often fell asleep over her work. Every time worry began to overpower her faith, she picked up the quilt her friends had prepared for her. If her friends' love and concern prompted them to give her a pleasant occupation while she battled for her health, she knew her heavenly Father was preparing and caring for her in an even better manner. The perfect gift not only supplied her need to feel usefully occupied during the long weeks of chemo, but viewing the handiwork of her friends buoyed up her emotional state. When her body was too weak to stitch, she sometimes sat and held the quilt as a tangible way to soak up her friends' love. Embracing the quilt reminded her of her friends and encouraged her to lean upon the strength of her best friend, Jesus.

Shasta used the summer after finishing her chemotherapy to complete the quilt. In addition to the pleasure the work gave her, she believes the project helped her face her illness with an attitude of faith.

God's Word urges us to help the weak. If we ask Him, He will show us creative ways to meet the needs of people when illness, finances, or heartbreak weaken them.

God's Pattern

The encouragement of others not only meets tangible needs, but it undergirds our attitudes, helping us sustain healthy thoughts when life seems to crumble around us. God did not design us to stand alone in times of trial.

Don't Forget Me

*For though I be absent in the flesh, yet am I
with you in the spirit, joying and beholding your
order, and the stedfastness of your faith in Christ.*
Colossians 2:5 KJV

"You're making another baby quilt? Who's pregnant in our church?" Angie, Melissa's neighbor, held the day's mail for both of them. She plopped into a chair.

"No one. This is for my niece's baby due in March." Melissa continued to appliqué the yellow duck on the pale green background.

"Why go to all that trouble? You'll never see her. She's never come to see you in Nevada, and she's not in Florida for you to see when you go home to visit."

"That's exactly the reason. Welcoming all the family babies connects me with family members I don't have a chance to see."

"They probably don't appreciate the trouble a quilt takes."

"Maybe not, but if I invest myself in my extended family, they'll grow to care about me. I think letters and acts of love enrich my life and theirs." Melissa bit off her thread and positioned a lamb next to the duck. "These family babies are going to grow up and become teenagers faced with all the difficult pressures teens experience today. Maybe knowing they have an aunt in Nevada who cares enough to make a quilt and send them cards will help make good choices. Pressure to live up to high family expectations never hurts a kid and can help a lot."

"One little quilt does all that! I don't think so." Angie leaned over to tap Melissa's knee with an envelope. "You're expecting too much mileage from your gift, even if it does represent a lot of work."

"Well, I always pray for the person when I make a quilt and when I send birthday and Christmas cards. I don't think prayers are ever wasted. By staying in touch with the family I may be able to contribute somehow to the next generation and their growth in the Lord." Melissa rested her work in her lap.

> **TIP**
> For a quilt square swap, each person in the group makes the same square enough times for every person to receive one. The squares are distributed, and everyone uses them to create her own quilt with a nice variety of squares and a lasting souvenir of each person.

"You don't actually get mail back from anyone, do you?" Angie's voice grew wistful. "All I get are advertisements." She showed Melissa the return address of a car dealer on her letter.

"I like feeling connected with my family even though I'm thousands of miles away surrounded by cattle and fir trees instead of relatives. I'm helping my own joy."

"I guess it was receiving only the usual junk mail that made me walk on over to your place. Do you think if I wrote someone in your family, they'd write me back?"

"I'll bet they would," Melissa answered, thinking, *I'll write to them first and tell them how much this isolated woman needs some mail.*

When Paul wrote to the Colossians, he used a phrase we often hear paraphrased. He wrote about being absent in the flesh but present in the spirit. That tie which joins our spirit with another person is worth establishing and maintaining.

God's Pattern

God is pleased when we make the effort to remain in
relationships with the people He plants in our lives.
We never know how our lives may impact people for
Christ because we have taken time for them. God can use
even small, infrequent contacts for good. Sometimes we
may never know how much our efforts mattered.

Where's the Pencil?

*For I know the thoughts that I think toward you,
saith the LORD, thoughts of peace,
and not of evil, to give you an expected end.*
JEREMIAH 29:11 KJV

*Where there is no vision, the people perish:
but he that keepeth the law, happy is he.*
PROVERBS 29:18 KJV

Does that look like the right height?" Kevin asked his wife, hammering two nails in the wall and hanging a dowel rod from them.

"I'll put the quilt on the rod, and we'll see." Vicky hung her wall hanging by its loops, rested the dowel on the nails, and stepped back to survey the effect. A chuckle turned into giggles and quickly grew into laughter. "Quick, hold up the wall before the quilt pulls it into the cellar!" Vicky ran to the wall and pretended to hold it up.

"It does look a little lopsided," Kevin said, examining

Vicky's face for any sign he shouldn't join in her merriment. After all, she had spent months making this quilt. He didn't want her to think he was laughing at it. But the more they looked, the funnier it became.

"All the dark colors are on one side and make it look like it's dragging the whole wall down." Vicky could hardly speak around her giggle attack.

"Are those two baskets of flowers supposed to be hanging upside down while the rest are faceup?" Kevin asked.

"Oh, I never noticed that before." Vicky sobered.

"Never mind." Kevin put his arms around her. "I like it because you made it."

TIP
Lay tiny pieces of material on paper to see in advance how a block will look. Rearrange the pieces until satisfied and then glue them in place as a reference.

She hugged him back. "Thanks, but you don't have to. I enjoyed doing it, so I'll just make another one. But this time I'll do what everyone told me I should do in the first place. Plan ahead. Got a pencil? I'll draw this as it ought to look and mark where I could change the colors so it doesn't look unbalanced."

Gorgeous quilts require planning. The pattern choice needs to fit the level of skill we've developed. The selection of fabric requires forethought for a pleasing blend and arrangement. A diagram to guide the arrangement of pieces provides a good checkpoint as the work progresses.

If we take the time to plan for good results with a quilt project, think how much more God planned when He created us. Ask God to show us His plan and our role in advancing His kingdom on earth.

God's Pattern

God is an excellent planner. His plans for us are designed for our good. He has held the blueprint for our lives from the moment of our conception.

SCRIPTURE INDEX

Old Testament

New Testament